THE REFERENCE SHELF

WOMEN IN THE MILITARY

Edited by E. A. Blacksmith

THE REFERENCE SHELF

Volume 64, Number 5

THE H. W. WILSON COMPANY

New York 1992

THE REFERENCE SHELF

The books in this series contain reprints of articles, excerpts from books, and addresses on current issues and social trends in the United States and other countries. There are six separately bound numbers in each volume, all of which are generally published in the same calendar year. One number is a collection of recent speeches; each of the others is devoted to a single subject and gives background information and discussion from various points of view, concluding with a comprehensive bibliography that contains books and pamphlets and abstracts of additional articles on the subject. Books in the series may be purchased individually or on subscription.

Library of Congress Cataloging-in-Publication Data

Women in the Military / edited by E. A. Blacksmith.
p. cm. — (The Reference shelf ; v. 64, no. 5)
Compilation of articles.
Includes bibliographical references

ISBN 0-8242-0829-3
1. United States—Armed Forces—Women. I. Blacksmith, E. A. II. Series.
UB418.W65W67 1992
355'.0082—dc20 92-34712
CIP

Cover: Saudi Arabia, Sept. 3—Portrait of a Bronx Warrior—U.S. Army Specialist Tanya Miller of the 101st Infantry Division who took part in Operation Desert Shield.
Photo: AP/Laser Photo/David Longstreath

Printed in the United States of America

CONTENTS

PREFACE 5

I. A WOMAN'S PREROGATIVE?

Editor's Introduction 7
Carolyn H. Becraft. Women and the Military: Bureaucratic Policies and Politics ....The Bureaucrat 8
Beverly Ann Bendekgey. Should Women Be Kept Out of Combat? .... The G.A.O. Journal 17
Lois B. DeFleur. Let Women Fly in Combat ....The Atlanta Constitution 24
Donald G. McNeil Jr. Should Women Be Sent Into Combat? ....The New York Times 26
Elaine Tyler May. Women in the Wild Blue Yonder ....The New York Times 32
Annette Fuentes. Women Warriors?: Equality, Yes—Militarism, No. .... The Nation 34
Charles Moskos. Army Women ...The Atlantic Monthly 40
Edward Norden. Right Behind You, Scarlett! .... The American Spectator 54

II. IN WHICH SHE SERVES: CAPABILITIES AND CHALLENGES

Editor's Introduction 62
Maj. Gen. Jeanne Holm. The Persian Gulf War. ....Women in the Military 63
Andrea Gross. Women Under Fire .... Ladies Home Journal 80
Barbara Kantrowitz. The Right to Fight .....Newsweek 86
Col. David H. Hackworth. War and the Second Sex ....Newsweek 89
Carol Barkalow. Women Have What It Takes ....Newsweek 96

Jeannie Ralston. Women's Work . . . . Life 99
98
Peter Cary and Bruce B. Auster. What's Wrong with the Navy? . . . . U.S. News & World Report 107

III. The Homefront Reaction

Editor's Introduction 115
Melinda Beck. Our Women in the Desert . . . . Newsweek 116
William F. Buckley Jr. Militarize Women? . . . . The National Review 122
Elaine Donnelly. What Did You Do in the Gulf, Mommy? . . . . The National Review 124
Florence King. Eve Fatigue . . . . . . The National Review 127
Anne Summers. Pat Schroeder: Fighting for Military Moms . . . . Ms. 129
Jean Bethke Elshtain. Feminism and War . . . . The Progressive 132
David Horowitz. The Feminist Assault on the Military . . . . The National Review 138
Julie Johnson. The New Top Guns . . . . Time 145
Richette L. Haywood. Should Moms Go To War? . . . Jet 146
Linda Bird Francke. Requiem for a Soldier . . . . The New York Times 150

Bibliography

Books and Pamphlets 154
Additional Periodical Articles with Abstracts 156

PREFACE

Since World War II women have served in the United States Armed Forces, but not until the Persian Gulf War has their role been subject to such public debate. Of course, this is partly due to the increased number of women serving. After the 1967 repeal of the limit on the number of women allowed to serve and the emergence of an all-volunteer force in 1973, it was probably only a matter of time before women soldiers would want the same chance as men to engage in the ultimate military experience, combat. Public debate on this point has been heated. The issue is not whether women have a place in the military, but rather, whether their services should or should not include combat duty from which they have always been excluded by either law or policy.

Those who favored an affirmative resolution to the debate were disappointed by the action of a Presidential commission in November 1992. Under the headline "Panel Rejects Major Role For Women in Combat," *The New York Times* wrote:

> With recommendations that seemed to turn more on social philosophy than military considerations, a Presidential commission delivered a resounding setback to supporters of an expanded role for women in the military.
>
> By an 8-to-7-vote, the panel said last week that women should continue to be barred from flying combat missions. It urged that women also be prohibited from engaging in ground combat. The panel did, however, recommend that women be allowed to serve on combat ships, though not on submarines or amphibious vessels.

The proper role of women in the military will, of course, continue to be a volatile issue not only in the armed services but also in the society at large. The question of whether America is willing to send its "nurturers" into battle is a complex controversy as the articles in this compilation amply attest.

Section one of this compilation explores the roles of women in the military, while describing the laws, policies and politics that exclude women from combat missions.

Section two looks more closely at the servicewomen themselves—their reasons for joining the military and their desire to serve in combat roles—from the patriotic to the pragmatic (advancement in the military is often predicated upon having combat experience). The articles in this section also discuss the struggle of military women to serve the needs of both home and career, while facing physical and mental hardships, sexual harassment, and job discrimination.

The final section of this compilation deals with the homefront, the effect women serving overseas have had on their families—parents, children, husbands. The commotion stirred by their decision to serve has also prompted reaction from supporters and detractors, peers and superiors and the American public.

The editor is grateful to the authors and publishers for permitting the reprinting of their material herein and a special note of thanks to the research staff of the H. W. Wilson Company, which collected, commented, and computerized this entire compilation.

E. A. Blacksmith

August 1992

I. A WOMAN'S PREROGATIVE?

EDITOR'S INTRODUCTION

As they adopt lifestyles in the 1990s that involve duties and responsibilities their mothers never dreamed of, American women continue to question their proper roles in every walk of life. In the civilian world of business their full participation is sometimes blocked by the so-called glass ceiling. In the armed forces, women encounter the combat exclusion rule, which some have dubbed the "brass ceiling."

In the first article of this section, Carolyn H. Becraft writing in *The Bureaucrat*, describes the rules and regulations governing the roles of women in the military and presents an outline of policies and political decisions, from the 1960s and 1970s up through the Carter and Reagan eras, charting how we have arrived at the current debate.

Next, Beverly Ann Bendekgey, writing in the U.S. General Accounting Office's quarterly, *The GAO Journal*, explores women's involvement in the Panama invasion and offers interpretation of the objectives of the combat exclusion laws. Ms. Bendekgey also questions whether rules that were made over forty years ago are applicable today and whether they have any real effect other than to limit opportunities to women.

The third article, by Lois B. DeFleur in *The Atlanta Constitution*, explains why the Gulf War made the participation of women soldiers seem so much more pronounced: "There were so many women whose involvement across a wide range of specialities put them where the action was."

The fourth article by Donald G. MacNeil, Jr. writing in *The New York Times*, discusses the "pros and cons" of women's involvement in warfare and the physical and psychological challenges women would have to face in various combat scenarios.

Elaine May Tyler, in an article from *The New York Times*, writes that the central issue in the women-as-combat-pilots debate is the notion "that women are the world's nurturers." The article goes on the contemplate whether they can be "destroyers" as well.

The sixth article of this section, by Annette Fuentes and reprinted from *The Nation*, looks at the "full integration of women into the voluntary service" and warily rejoices at the Senate vote to "eliminate regulations that prohibit women in the Air Force and Navy from flying combat missions." Ms. Fuentes also writes of the division of opinion among military women themselves over the combat exclusion rule.

The next article, written by Charles Moskos and reprinted from *The Atlantic Monthly*, is based on the author's interviews with "soldiers of every rank who participated in the invasion of Panama, including most of the women soldiers who were closest to the shooting." Their sentiments and aspirations—including for some, combat are covered in depth.

The final article of this section, by Edward Norden from *The American Spectator*, considers the debate from the point of view of an Israeli whose country has already dealt with the issue of women in combat. While acknowledging inherent differences between the U.S. Armed Forces and those of Israel where "the 'right to fight' won't remain an abstract one for long," the author remains skeptical about the morality of a society that allows this as a commonplace practice.

WOMEN AND THE MILITARY: BUREAUCRATIC POLICIES AND POLITICS[1]

Change in any bureaucratic organization is difficult. When the policy changes affect the fundamental values of the organization, the resistance to change is likely to be very intense and require constant monitoring over long periods of time in order to ensure implementation. One such case in recent years has been the emotional public policy dilemma for politicians and for the Department of Defense (DOD) regarding the expanded role of women in the military.

[1]Article by Carolyn H. Becraft, a research associate with Decision Resources Corporation, Washington, DC. This article is based on a paper prepared for the 5th Annual Women and Work Conference, University of Texas at Arlington, May 12-13, 1988. Portions of it appeared as "The Personnel Puzzle" in the Spring 1989 issue of Naval Proceedings. Reprinted from *The Bureaucrat*, Fall 1989, 33-36. Reprinted by permission.

While insisting that they won't stand for women in combat, politicians in both political parties, motivated by the reality of the declining pool of males eligible for military service, have been responsible, however reluctantly, for pushing DOD to expand the numbers of and roles for military women. DOD has reacted to this external pressure by trying to reaffirm the institutional culture, values, and traditions that have served to justify its exclusionary practices.

Political and Legal Decisions

The rise in the percentage of women in the military and the growing number of career fields open to them are the direct result of political and legal decisions over the past 20 years. Three specific political decisions were crucial:

- the elimination of ceilings on the grades and numbers of military women in 1967;
- the end of the male draft in 1973, resulting in the All Volunteer Force; and
- the opening of the military academies to women in 1976.

Three court decisions were also significant. Significant impediments to the retention of military women were removed by the *Frontiero v. Richardson* [1973] ruling that dependents of military women could receive the same entitlements as those offered for the dependents of military men and by the *Crawford v. Cushman* [1976] decision that a woman could not be discharged if she became pregnant or if she had dependents less than 18 years old. A third decision, *Owens v. Brown* [1978], forced the Navy to open certain categories of ships for assignment to women.

The Carter Years

As a result of these decisions—particularly the commitment to the All Volunteer Force—plus a 1977 Brookings Institution study which proposed that the services increase the numbers of women in order to reduce their requirements for men, there was concerted pressure on the services from DOD political officials in the Carter administration to expand opportunities for women in the military. The Brookings report also pointed out that such a shift would be more cost-effective because women were less expensive to recruit than men.

Tasked to evaluate the potential for utilizing increased numbers of women, the military departments countered that this issue was not one of cost-effectiveness, but rather of combat-effectiveness. They argued that women tend to be weaker than men, limiting the work that they could do. They also argued that combat exclusion laws for the Navy and Air Force, in conjunction with the exclusion policies for the Army, further restricted the kinds of work [women] could do.

Subsequently, even when internal DOD analysts reported that the services could utilize far more women, the military departments resisted with arguments ranging from concerns about rotation base formulas to concerns about men and women housed in the same building. At the same time, the Army conducted two research studies during combat exercises in an effort to determine a level at which the addition of women to a unit resulted in *decreased* combat readiness. Instead, the results of both studies indicated that women performed well with the units and that the key to a unit's performance was not the male/female ratio, but the quality of leadership.

Current Status of Military Women

The percentage of women in the military has increased dramatically, from less than two percent at the beginning of the All Volunteer Force in 1973 to eight percent in 1980. By 1987, the percentage of women the military had risen to 10.2 percent. By 1988 over 220,000 officers and enlisted women were serving in the military, many in nontraditional "combat-type" jobs such as pilots, security police, truck drivers, and missile gunners.

Women have participated actively in military missions, as well. In the 1983 Grenada invasion, Air Force women flew aircraft that delivered supplies and equipment to U.S. forces, and Army women, serving in a variety of combat support roles, were present from the second day of the invasion. In 1986, Navy women pilots performed carrier landings as a part of the antiterrorism operation against Libya, and Air Force women pilots were a part of the crews that provided combat support to the fighter planes that attacked Libya. In 1987, when the *U.S.S. Acadia* was sent to the Persian Gulf to repair damage done to the frigate *U.S.S. Stark,* 25 percent of the crew of the *U.S.S. Acadia* were women.

Combat Exclusion Laws and Policies

There is no U.S. law that prevents women from serving in combat. There are, however, statutory provisions precluding the permanent assignment of Air Force and Navy women to duty on certain types of platforms in certain conditions or "situations." In the Air Force, women are prohibited from duty in aircraft engaged in combat missions. There is, however, a "Catch 22"—women in medical, dental, chaplain, and other "professional" categories are exempt from this restriction. Currently, only the offensive fighter, bomber, and selected reconnaissance planes are designated as combat aircraft; therefore, approximately 97 percent of Air Force jobs should technically be available for assignment to women.

Navy women are prohibited from permanent assignment on vessels or aircraft that can be expected to engage in combat missions. The responsibility for the designation of "combat" mission has been left up to the Navy. Navy women can be assigned to support aircraft, repair ships, and . . . to certain support ships in the Combat Logistics Force [December 1987]. The other seagoing service, the Coast Guard, which is a part of the Department of Transportation, has no restrictions on the utilization of women.

The Marine Corps, part of the Department of the Navy, is the most restrictive of the services in utilizing women. In addition to being governed by the constraints of the Navy, the Marines further restrict women from serving in combat units or combat situations as designated by the Corps.

Unlike the Air Force and the Navy, which have statutory restrictions on the utilization of women, the Army has no such legal constraints. In fact, the secretary of the Army has the statutory authority to determine the assignment policies for all soldiers. In 1977, at the request of Congress and prior to the termination of the Women's Army Corps in 1978, the Army developed a combat exclusion policy that resulted in the classification of 38 enlisted job categories as "combat" jobs unavailable to women.

The Reagan Era

In December 1980, in a veiled attempt to bolster support to resurrect the draft, the Army and Air Force approached the Reagan transition team with complaints that the previous administration [that of President Carter] had forced them to increase unduly the number of women in their services. Senior military officials, with the acquiescence of certain sympathetic politicians, justified their plans to cut back on the recruitment of enlisted women. They argued that, since women did not have the degree of upper body strength of men, the real performance of women in military units was unknown; that the armed forces should not be an instrument of social change; and that the services should only reflect the social mores of civilian society. Thus, in their view, increased numbers of women would be detrimental to the military's mission as well as result in social upheaval in military units. The arguments given and the tactics used were remarkably similar to the institutional resistance of the military departments to racial integration 25 years earlier.

Shifting Interpretations of Laws and Policies

The Army

The Army then formed a study group to evaluate the policies concerning women in the Army. Among the results of the policy review was the decision to close 23 additional job categories to women. This decision, which directly affected 1,200 women, also had an adverse impact on the career progression of over 15,000 Army women.

Almost immediately, the Army came under heavy criticism for the hypothesis and methodology used in the policy review. Critics included manpower specialists, commanders in the field, retired military women, advocacy groups, Congress, and the secretary of defense's own Defense Advisory Committee on Women in the Services (DACOWITS). In 1985, after a review directed by the secretary of the army, many of the job categories closed in 1982 were reopened. At present, 52 percent of all Army slots are potentially open to assignment of women.

The Air Force

The Air Force has always been the most vulnerable to outside political pressure to increase opportunities for women. In 1981, only seven percent of all Air Force jobs were classified as combat jobs and therefore closed to women. As of 1988 the percentage dwindled to three percent. Unable to justify exclusion of women on "combat" grounds, the Air Force designed an accession methodology that would assure that the female content of the Air Force would not exceed the 1981 level of 11.5 percent. The resultant "propensity to enlist" factor, which automatically reduced the eligible female population to be recruited by three-fourths, came under scrutiny from the House Armed Services Committee in 1983. Since 1985 Congress has closely monitored the Air Force's female accessions, and the percentage of women has risen to approximately 12.6 percent of the total Air Force.

THE NAVY AND MARINE CORPS

In the early 1980s, the Navy was implementing its Women in Ships Program, developed in 1978, and had begun to assign women to certain auxiliary ships—primarily shore-based repair ships and certain research ships—as required by law. Attention was next directed toward expanding seagoing opportunities for women on an additional category of auxiliary ships, the logistics ships of the Military Sealift Command (MSC) and the Navy's Mobile Logistics Support Force (MLSF). The Navy prohibited military women from assignment opportunities in military detachments on the civilian MSC ships, even though civilian women were routinely assigned to these ships.

When the secretary of defense directed the Navy to open the detachments on MSC ships for assignment of Navy women in 1984, the Navy began the process internally of changing the name of the MLSF to the Combat Logistics Force in an apparent attempt to include those ships in the provision of the Navy's combat exclusion law, thereby shielding them from permanent assignment of women. Meanwhile, in the Marine Corps, the most tradition-bound of the services, the numbers and positions available for women, with new exceptions, changed very little.

Inconsistencies Among the Services

Not only are there different statutory provisions for each military department, but, in addition, the various departments are not consistent in their policies.Women can be pilots in all of the services except the Marine Corps. Civilian women have served regularly on civilian ships, while positions on selected comparable Navy ships in the Combat Logistics Force have only recently been opened to Navy women. All positions in the Coast Guard have been open to women since 1978, yet in time of war Coast Guard ships come under control of the Navy, which limits opportunities for women at sea. Army women hold critical positions present in the forward support areas of the battlefield, in contrast to the Marine Corps women, who primarily serve in rear area personnel and administrative functions.

Role of Public Opinion

Another aspect of the political dimension in the expansion of roles for military women is public support. Arguments against increasing opportunities and roles for women in the military invariably begin with concerns about the "will of the American people." Evidence suggests, however, that the public is quite comfortable with nontraditional roles for military women. A poll conducted in August 1986 by NBC News found that 52 percent of the public supported women in combat support roles, and 77 percent were comfortable with the current policy that military women will not be evacuated in a military conflict.

This coincides with a 1982 poll by the National Opinion Research Center which measured support for women in specific jobs. According to these data, 84 percent of the American public supported keeping or increasing the proportion of women in the services, and 94 percent approved of women nurses in a combat zone. The approval rate for military women in combat support jobs was equally high: 83 percent as military truck mechanics and 73 percent as jet transport pilots. Concerning military jobs specifically involving offensive combat roles, 62 percent supported the idea of women as jet fighter pilots, 59 percent as missile gunners, 57 percent as crew members on a combat ship, and 35 percent as participants in hand-to-hand combat.

Senior military officials remain apprehensive, however, about public acceptance of women in nontraditional military roles. Some voice concerns that men will be reluctant to fight if women are present, and, although acknowledging that women will be among the casualties in any major conflict, they worry about the effect of the women returning in body bags. Yet results of military missions in the 1980s such as the Air Force attack against Libya, missions in Grenada and Honduras, and the Navy's repair mission of the frigate damaged in the Persian Gulf—all of which utilized military women—show no reported negative effects on the performance of the men involved.

Similarly, to date, women casualties on civilian police forces, the very public deaths of women astronauts on the shuttle Challenger in 1986, the deaths of Army women in the Gander crash in 1986, and the Navy woman fatality in the terrorist bombing of a USO club in Italy in 1988 have failed to spark public controversy.

Intervention of Secretary of Defense and Service Secretaries

During the initial relaxation of political pressure on the services at the beginning of the Reagan administration, the military departments attempted to minimize the extent of organizational change created by the insistence of the previous political administration to integrate women. Inevitably, the service secretaries and the secretary of defense have had to reassert themselves and intervene to stop attempts to restrict or eliminate opportunities, and have subsequently directed their respective departments to increase opportunities for military women.

- The secretary of the Army directed the Army to reevaluate its decision to close additional job categories in 1983, resulting in the reopening of most of the job categories in 1985.
- The Air Force secretary reopened the security police force in 1984, and opened the peacekeeper missile field in 1985, as well as certain reconnaissance aircraft roles in 1987.
- In 1984, the secretary of defense announced that the military detachments on civilian ships that deploy with the battlegroup would be open to assignment for Navy women.
- In 1987, the secretary of the Navy, ending a two-year internal debate on this issue, opened opportunities on certain support ships in the Combat Logistics Force.
- In 1988, the secretary of defense, over the objections of the commandant of the Marine Corps, opened positions in the embassy security guard program to women.

Future Issues

Because of projected recruiting difficulties resulting from the shrinking pool of eligible males for military service, attention will remain focused on the need for additional sources for recruits, including women. In addition, the Defense Advisory Committee on Women in the Services and others have expressed concern that the varying interpretations of the combat exclusion laws and policies by the services have resulted in inconsistencies in the types of positions available for women, as well as a shortage of career opportunities for qualified mid-career women. In an effort to ease these conditions, and to prod the services further, legislation was introduced in the U.S. House and Senate in 1987 to require all services to open thousands of combat support jobs to women.

Although the rise in the percentage of women in the military since the beginning of the All Volunteer Force will probably level off, the declining pool of eligible male recruits, coupled with the mutual desire of Congress and the Department of Defense to maintain the quality of the recruits attained in recent years, and the political unwillingness to return to the all-male draft, will continue to influence the necessity to recruit women. In addition, the increasing numbers of women vying for the more prestigious mid-level and senior positions will force additional scrutiny on the services' interpretation of combat exclusion laws as well as the culture and traditions of the military, in order to provide continued career progression for women.

A related phenomenon has also been occurring in government agencies and the civilian corporate sector with increasing numbers of professional women in mid-level positions hitting a "glass ceiling" of institutional tradition, culture, and values which hinders their elevation to upper-level management positions.

Military women's competence and performance as individuals has been hesitantly acknowledged internally since 1980. Women are promoted at a faster rate than their male contemporaries. The focus of internal resistance appears to be shifting to lifestyle issues which affect women as a group, such as pregnancy and parental leave policies, accommodations to the needs of dual-career couples, and a perceived institutional reluctance to deal effectively and convincingly with the issue of gender harassment. While these issues are organizational issues, because of the relatively small numbers of women they tend to be cast in terms of "problems" for the institution caused by women instead of the results of the reluctance of the organization to adjust to changing structural conditions.

Summary and Conclusion

Tradition and military culture, the realities of changing demographics, constrained opportunities for military women, and the needs of the All Volunteer Force are all factors converging upon each other to perpetuate tension in the armed services. The quality and skills of military women contribute increasingly to sustaining the readiness of the U.S. military. Yet, as is typical with patterns of organizational stress, forces within the military departments can be expected to continue to employ countermeasures in an effort to limit both the numbers of military women and the opening of more significant military positions to women, in an effort to maintain the traditional culture of the organization.

In order to assure continued assimilation of women in the military, it will continue to be necessary for civilian political officials in the Department of Defense and Congress to provide guidance and oversight of the military in the interest of equitable treatment of military women and preservation of the effectiveness of the All Volunteer Force.

SHOULD WOMEN BE KEPT OUT OF COMBAT?[2]

During the U.S. military action in Panama [December 1989], a platoon of military police exchanged gunfire with Panamanian soldiers at an attack-dog compound near Panama City. This incident was nothing out of the ordinary—except that the U.S. platoon was led by a woman, making this the first modern instance of American women engaging hostile troops in combat. Current laws and regulations exclude women from direct combat roles, but there has been a long-standing debate—reopened by the recent events in Panama—over whether these exclusions should be maintained.

[2]Article by Beverly Ann Bendekgey, a senior evaluator in the Manpower Issue Area in G.A.O.'s National Security and International Affair Division. From *The G.A.O. Journal*, 9:29–33, Summer 1990. Reprinted by permission.

The laws governing women's role in the armed forces have been on the books for more than 40 years. To recognize the contribution that women made to the military during World War II, Congress passed the Women's Armed Services Integration Act of 1948, which authorized career opportunities for women in the regular and reserve forces. The act made it possible, for the first time, for women to pursue military careers; it also included several restrictions, including what are known as the combat exclusion laws. Today these combat exclusion laws prohibit the assignment of women to aircraft or naval vessels engaged in combat missions. (Because the Women's Army Corps existed until 1978 and had its own restrictions, there was no need in 1948 for statutes covering the Army).

In the 42 years since the Women's Armed Services Integration Act was passed, many significant changes have occurred that raise serious questions about the extent to which combat exclusion laws can be effectively applied. For one thing, the number of women in the military has soared to nearly 11 percent of all forces, a result largely of the removal in 1967 of the 2-percent ceiling on women in the military and the switch in 1973 from a draft to an all-volunteer force. This increase in the number of women has meant that a greater proportion of military personnel are barred from fully participating in military action. In addition, a general expansion of professional opportunities for women—both military and civilian—has encouraged frequent challenges to the job restrictions imposed by the combat exclusion laws. Finally, dramatic changes in communication and weapons technology have significantly altered the way wars are fought, blurring distinctions between combat and noncombat roles and between safe versus high-risk areas.

The laws' rationale

The existing combat exclusion laws do not directly address the issue of prohibiting women from engaging in combat. What they say is: Women shall not be assigned to Air Force and Navy aircraft or naval vessels "engaged in combat missions." The statutes neither state their underlying objectives nor define "combat mission."

In implementing the laws, the services have tried to fill these gaps. For one thing, they have tried to determine what might be the laws' unspoken objectives. Possible interpretations of these include: to address concerns about women's ability to "fight," to codify attitudes about what roles are considered "acceptable" for women, and to protect women from hazards of war.

In addition, the services have established definitions of what constitutes a combat mission. The Air Force, for example, defines combat mission aircraft as those whose principal mission is to deliver munitions against an enemy. Women, therefore, cannot serve on fighter or bomber aircraft, such as the F-4, the F-16, and the B-52. Because the Air Force interprets the law as intended to protect women, it closes other assignments to them on the basis of risk of exposure to hostile fire and capture. Fighter reconnaissance aircraft such as the RF-4, for instance, are closed to women because their usual mission is to fly over enemy territory before and after attacks.

The Navy defines combat mission aircraft and vessels as those that seek out, reconnoiter, and engage the enemy. Accordingly, women may not be permanently assigned to such ships as destroyers, submarines, and aircraft carriers, or to the aircraft associated with carriers. In addition, because an aircraft carrier task force can have a mission as a group, the supply ships that routinely travel with the carrier group are also closed to women.

The restrictions that the Navy imposes also apply to the Marine Corps, which does not assign women to units that will deploy on combat mission ships or direct combat units. Marine Corps policy does acknowledge, however, that women may be assigned to support roles that could become engaged in defensive combat during an enemy attack.

Although the role of women in the Army is not covered by statute, the Army bases its assignment policy for women on its interpretation of the intent of the laws for the Air Force and the Navy. Women in the Army may not be assigned to those jobs most likely to engage them in direct combat, the risk of which is assessed on the basis of job duties, unit mission, tactical doctrine, and battlefield location. Battlefield location, according to Army officials, has the greatest impact on this risk assessment. As a result, women are excluded not only from direct combat positions but also from some combat support positions that are expected to be near the front line.

Until recently, the services used different risk levels to identify the noncombat positions that would be closed to women. In

1988, however, the Department of Defense standardized the criterion for identifying which noncombat positions may be closed. The risk rule, as it is called, assumes that protecting women is an objective of the combat exclusion laws. The rule states that women should be excluded only from those noncombat positions that are exposed to risk that is equal to or greater than that faced by associated combat units. The immediate impact of the risk rule was to open several thousand more positions to women.

Problems and inconsistencies

The services have made extensive efforts to apply the combat exclusion laws appropriately and effectively. But the changes in warfare that have occurred since 1948 raise questions about whether that goal is achievable. Despite several revisions in service policies, women are still barred from some fighting positions but not from others, protected (to varying degrees) in some positions but highly exposed to danger in others, and allowed to perform some tasks not traditionally assigned to women while prohibited from performing others.

Consider, for example, the impact that the laws have on a woman in the Air Force. She may "deliver munitions" against an enemy by firing a land-based missile from U.S. or European soil—but she may *not* deliver munitions from an F-16. The restriction seems designed to "protect" this woman. But it's difficult to judge which of these two positions is actually exposed to the greater danger; land-based missiles, after all, would be targets in the event of war. Furthermore, the degree to which a woman is "protected" in either situation depends not just on U.S. capabilities but also on enemy capabilities—something beyond this country's control.

The Navy provides another example of the difficulties inherent in applying the combat exclusion laws. Naval vessels include 37 combat logistics force supply ships. Of these, 24 normally shuttle between storage depots and the ships being supplied, while 13 usually travel continuously with a battle group, such as an aircraft carrier task force. In December 1987, the Navy announced that it would admit women to the 24 shuttle supply ships. Women would still be excluded, however, from the 13 supply ships that travel with battle groups, since these ships share the battle groups' missions. Application of the Defense Department's risk rule sustained this decision, since the 13 supply ships that travel with battle groups were judged as being exposed to the same degree of danger as the ships within that group.

Since these supply ships are not, in themselves, combat mission ships, the only purpose for closing them would seem to be to protect women. It is difficult to determine, however, which supply ships are more exposed to danger—those that travel with battle groups and therefore can avail themselves of the protection of, say, an aircraft carrier task force, or those that travel back and forth between combat groups and storage depots. A risk assessment is made all the more sensitive by current military strategies and tactics, which increasingly emphasize attacking supply lines as a way of decreasing an enemy's fighting capacity.

The combat exclusion laws may have originated in part from concerns about women's ability to fight. This may make sense in the cases of the Army and the Marine Corps, some of whose members are expected to be able to engage in hand-to-hand combat requiring a level of physical strength that, some would say, women are not generally capable of attaining. But the laws themselves explicitly close aircraft and ships, where there would be little if any dispute about women's capabilities. Furthermore, the Marine Corps now includes defensive combat in basic training for women; one wonders why, if women can be trained for defensive combat, they cannot also be trained for offensive combat. The U.S. military action in Panama also highlights the difficulty in clearly defining combat and noncombat roles in today's military environment; as mentioned earlier, the debate over whether Army women were or were not in combat in Panama centered on the responsibilities and actions of military police units containing women.

As long as assignments for women produce these varying results, the apparent objectives of the exclusion laws are not being fulfilled. Perhaps they cannot be fulfilled. If the laws' objectives *are* indeed unattainable, then the primary effect of the laws seems only to be an arbitrary limitation of opportunities for women in the armed services.

Possible revisions

The Defense Department's risk rule, which stipulates that only those noncombat positions involving risks as great as those experienced in associated combat positions should be closed to women, represented one attempt to iron out inconsistencies in the implementation of the combat exclusion laws. An earlier attempt was made in 1987, when Senator William Cohen and former Senator William Proxmire introduced legislation that would have barred women only from "fighting" positions, thereby opening all noncombat positions regardless of their exposure to danger. The bill died without a hearing.

Both these efforts raise continuing questions about the feasibility of establishing a workable law for keeping women out of combat. It is not clear that excluding military women from some combat and noncombat jobs really provides them with an added degree of protection. For one thing, it is difficult to define a context in which *anyone* in today's military can be protected from the dangers of war. And, as was evident in Panama, civilians are at as much risk as military personnel. Furthermore, although the risk rule's basic criterion seems sensible, it may not provide the same degree of protection across the services because of different ways in which the services fight.

Consider, for example, the contrasts between a Navy aircraft carrier task force and an Air Force base in Europe. No women may be assigned to any of the ships in an aircraft carrier task force because the group, by definition, has a combat mission. (As mentioned earlier, application of the risk rule supported the closing of the supply ships that travel with the carrier group.) Many women could be stationed, however, at a U.S. air base in Europe. The main task of a carrier task force is the launching of the carrier's aircraft, and the main task of a U.S. air base is the launching of its aircraft. The Navy unit moves; the Air Force unit is landlocked. Both units have ways of defending themselves from enemy attack. Both would be primary targets in a war. Is one unit at higher risk of attack than the other? Is one unit more vulnerable than the other? Are Navy women afforded more protection than Air Force women? These questions are difficult, perhaps impossible, to answer.

The Cohen/Proxmire bills' dismissal of protection as an objective of the combat exclusion laws raises the question: Is it logical to close positions that women may be capable of filling if they can, by law, still be exposed to the greatest risks? For example, under the current law, the Air Force allows women to fly the tankers that refuel (in the air) the long-distance F-111 bomber—

the aircraft used in the attack on Libya. If the tanker is shot down before it gets to the bomber, the bomber cannot reach its target. Many people would argue that the tanker faces a risk of attack at least as great as that faced by the bomber. If protection is ruled out as an objective of the combat exclusion laws, what is the rationale for prohibiting qualified women from flying the bomber? What is the rationale for closing nearly 6,000 positions on an aircraft carrier if only a small fraction of that number actually crew the aircraft?

The law's effects

The continued existence of the combat exclusion laws for women denies the services the opportunity to most efficiently and effectively manage their human resources. For instance, because combat mission aircraft are closed to Air Force women, the number of women who can enter pilot training is limited; this may result in highly qualified women being passed over for less qualified men. . . . December's [1989] military action in Panama provides another example: the 82nd Airborne Division, deploying from Fort Bragg, North Carolina, left behind a woman intelligence analyst whose area of expertise was Panama.

The exclusion laws also close jobs that provide experience crucial for promotion—especially at the higher and general officer grades. Women have less opportunity, therefore, to continue to the military and to further their own professional development. This may help explain why, at career decision points, women are more likely to leave the service than men are.

In sum, problems seen inherent in the implementation of any kind of combat exclusions in today's warfare environment. Moreover, the existing combat exclusions limit the military's ability to manage its forces and to fully utilize its human resources. In light of these problems, one must question whether combat exclusion provisions are feasible or are in the military's best interest.

LET WOMEN FLY IN COMBAT[3]

The debate over whether or not women should fly combat missions now under way in Congress has more to do with images than reality.

There is the image of the hypothetical woman in the trenches locked bayonet-to-bayonet with a stronger and deadly enemy sketched by Gen. H. Norman Schwarzkopf when he testified on Capitol Hill recently.

There is the image of Maj. Marie T. Rossi, a helicopter pilot assigned to fly supplies to troops in the combat zone of the Gulf War, killed in a fatal crash the day after the cease-fire. Major Rossi had come to personalize the war and the role of women in it for millions of CNN viewers.

There is the image of Spec. Melissa Rathbun-Healy, only 20 years old, captured on a supply mission that came under fire near the Saudi Arabian border. Specialist Rathbun-Healy, the first servicewoman since World War II to be made a prisoner of war, was also among the first 10 Americans released after the war by the Baghdad government.

And, finally, there were the indelible pictures that we saw on magazine covers and on television of gulf-bound mothers tearfully leaving behind at home uncomprehending toddlers.

These images arouse powerful emotional reactions. But we should not permit these responses to cloud our judgment about whether women should fly Navy, Air Force and Marine warplanes in combat. This is no time to sound a retreat on the gains that women have made in every one of the services since the Vietnam War.

Women have always been present on the battlefield. Some have borne weapons in their own defense and that of their homes. Personal heroism and courage were hallmarks of generations of American nurses and other support personnel who served in field hospitals and behind the lines from the Civil War to Vietnam.

[3]Article by Lois B. DeFleur, a pilot, and president of the State University of New York. Article appeared in *The Atlanta Constitution*, Jl 1, 1991. ©1991 *The Atlanta Constitution*. Reprinted with permission from *The Atlanta Journal* and *The Atlanta Constitution*.

What was distinctive about the Gulf War was that, for the first time, there were so many women whose involvement across a wide range of specialties put them where the action was.

The 35,000 women among the 540,000 troops sent to the Persian Gulf who were maintaining vehicles, servicing fighter planes, carrying supplies, and monitoring communications did not arrive there by accident.

The armed services had recruited and trained them in unprecedented numbers throughout the '70s and '80s. A commitment by the military to equal opportunity carried with it the possibility that women would necessarily be thrust into perilous situations.

As have countless men before them, these women had chosen military service as a way out of the traditional paths open to them. They were looking for technical training, college money, medical benefits, travel and adventure. "The Army was a starting block for her," a friend of Specialist Rathbun-Healy said in an interview when she was captured. "She had everything to look forward to."

My research and that of others supports this view. Women who have served in the military have a higher self-image than do their sisters who have remained in the pink-collar ghetto.

In addition, military pay and benefit structures surpass what women with similar educational backgrounds and opportunities are able to command in the civilian workplace. Men and women in the armed services are paid equally for equal work—a pattern not duplicated elsewhere.

When women complete their military service, they return to the work force with training in many fields that have been traditionally inhospitable to women. Especially in today's high-tech military, this training is very likely to open the doors to jobs in aviation, electronics, transportation and communications that are higher-paying than those held by women in more "traditional" female jobs.

But as long as promotions to military leadership positions rest largely on performance in battle, women will be at a disadvantage in achieving high ranks if they are not involved in combat.

Without successful role models up and down the military hierarchy, women in the service are destined to feel like second-class citizens.

Whether women should fly combat planes is a strategic, not a political, judgment. An enemy will never know whether a man or a woman is at the controls of an F-15.

The qualities that a successful combat pilot requires today are not gender-specific. The technologically sophisticated warplanes of the '90s make far more demands on a pilot's ability to manipulate complex computer programs and to make clear-headed tactical decisions than they do on sheer physical strength.

As the Gulf War demonstrated, not all battles are fought in the trenches. If a woman can fly a helicopter filled with ammunition to the front or pilot refueling tankers, it is difficult to see why she could not fly the F-4 or F-15 combat aircraft.

There is a very thin line between a woman engaged in duty in the combat zone and one actually engaged in combat duty.

Women have derived significant benefits from the career and educational opportunities made available to them in recent years by the armed services. In turn, the military has been enriched by the talent, hard work and dedication of the young women in its ranks.

The Air Force currently leads the way in utilizing women throughout its ranks and among its specialties. This policy should be continued and expanded so that women who are trained in aviation in all the service branches can fully serve the nation.

SHOULD WOMEN BE SENT INTO COMBAT?[4]

EXPOSURE to danger is not combat. Being shot at, even being killed, is not combat. Combat is finding . . . closing with . . . and killing or capturing the enemy. It's KILLING. And it's done in an environment that is often as difficult as you can possibly imagine. Extremes of climate. Brutality. Death. Dying. It's . . . uncivilized! And women CAN'T DO IT! Nor should they even be thought of as doing it. The requirements for strength and endurance render them UNABLE to do it. And I may be old-fashioned, but I think the very nature of women disqualifies them from doing it. Women give life. Sustain life. Nurture life. They don't TAKE it.

That Congressional testimony last month [June 1991] by Gen. Robert H. Barrow, who retired in 1983 as Commandant of the Marine Corps, suggests what women who want to fight may have to confront first.

[4]Article by Donald G. McNeil Jr., from *The New York Times*, Jl 21, 1991, E:3.

General Barrow's presentation was impassioned, but he delivered the same message to the Senate Armed Services Committee as the more rhetorically cautious service chiefs and as two female sergeants, one from the Marines and one from the 82d Airborne: the chiefs don't want women to fight, and many enlisted women don't want to either.

The issue has been raised partly because the war in the gulf—and General Barrow was scoffing at claims that women were baptized in combat there—led to an amendment to a military budget bill that would allow, but not require, the Air Force, Navy and Marines to let women pilots fly combat missions. The Army is governed by policy, not law, but would probably follow suit. The House has passed the bill. The Senate committee voted July 11 to study the amendment further and not vote on it until 1993. If the full Senate agrees, the two houses must work out their differences in conference on the bill this fall.

Defenders of letting women fill combat jobs say the services now hew to a paternalistic and inequitable policy: not keeping servicewomen from getting killed, but still not letting them kill. They argue that killing is what the military does, meaning the top ranks are nearly closed to those who don't at least learn the trade. If qualified women, they say, are allowed to be surgeons, astronauts and Supreme Court Justices—and military police and instructor pilots—then they ought to be able to lead rifle companies and strafe tank columns.

First Barriers Are In the Air

If the barriers fall, they will do so first in the air, where no heavy lifting is required and some women already train men as combat pilots. Then presumably some combat ships—even the redoubtable Royal Navy has women aboard theirs. Artillery may be next, since missile artillery is now open to women, and it is a specialty few men request; only one graduate of the last West Point class did. But other ground combat jobs, where strength and endurance matter in decisions like "Can this platoon carry a 52-pound mortar and enough 5-pound rounds to make it worth carrying?" may wait a long time.

The pressure to open the ranks is coming largely from pilots, most of whom are officers, and there is little clamor from enlisted women. Nor is there a pressing military need. Nor a civilian [illegible]swell. "I get a letter a day from clergymen saying we ought [illegible]nge our policy on homosexuals," Michael P. W. Stone, Secret[illegible] of the Army, said last week. "I don't get a letter a month saying we ought to change it on women." At the same time, in contrast to General Barrow, he said he thought that physical differences, even for the infantry, were "irrelevant," that the services could "design around the limitations."

But he did not favor easing standards. Basic training has easier tests for women, and women go to parachute school. But they are not allowed in advanced combat training, like Ranger school—considered a "ticket punch" to higher rank even for officers in specialties like intelligence or logistics—where jungle and desert warfare is taught on long sleepless exercises with heavy equipment. Nor do women become SEALs, whose six months of training include 14-mile races by seven-man teams carrying telephone poles and ocean swims while hog-tied.

Since Canada opened its infantry course to women in 1989, under orders from a human rights tribunal, only one of 102 women has passed.

Equal Opportunity

Opening combat to women also raises a thorny civil rights issue. Equal opportunity is not the same in the military as it is in civilian life—where no one actually forces you to, say, take a job or sit at a lunch counter. When pressed, commanders can take any soldier in any specialty, except chaplains and medics, and make him a rifleman. In wartime, infantry units often must be filled that way. If combat jobs are opened to women officers who want them, courts citing the equal protection doctrine would presumably rule that women who *don't* want them are eligible for transfer too, just as men are.

Two female officers who testified before Senator John Glenn's subcommittee on defense manpower said that risk is part of signing up to defend your country. The two sergeants said many women would think about quitting instead. Recruiters might face a nightmare. The services prize their enlisted women, who have more education, initially get promoted faster, and even when pregnancy leave is included, take less time off than men, who lose it to sports and auto injuries and drug, alcohol and discipline problems.

Proponents of letting women fill some combat jobs recall the aphorisms that were once used to keep blacks out of them, to wit, that they would run, could not follow orders, and were psychologically unequipped to lead whites. Only through integration under Truman did such notions get refuted. Women, they argue, deserve the same chance.

For and Against Changing the Rules

Jets

Women may fly transports, refueling tankers, Awacs, high-altitude reconnaissance. They may not fly fighters or bombers, or electronic jammers or reconnaissance planes in combat.

Critics Say: Combat pilots operate deep in enemy territory and are often shot down or captured. Some pilots have to cross-train as forward air controllers—joining infantry to coordinate air strikes. The job is grueling—80 percent of the men who take Air Force training for it wash out.

Proponents Say: Many women can "pull G's"— stand quick turns without blacking out—as well as men. Weapons are fired by pushing buttons. Women are already combat-qualified instructors on fighters, attend "Top Gun"-type schools, test new jets and missiles, land on aircraft carriers and train men to fly combat missions. Without time in combat wings, women lose promotion opportunities. They are "in combat" since Awacs and tankers are prime targets. Women fly fighters in Canada's Air Force.

Helicopters

Women now ferry troops, fuel and ammunition into enemy territory and fly missions to evacuate wounded. They may not fly Apache or Cobra gunships or the Kiowa scout helicopters that direct gunship fire and let commanders hover over battlefields.

Critics: Like jets, helicopters operate deep in enemy territory, so pilots risk death or capture.

Proponents: Women are already helicopter test pilots. They fly medical evacuation flights—among the most dangerous, since the enemy is often waiting to ambush them. Gunships, by contrast, are heavily armored and rely on surprise.

Ships

Women are allowed on supply and repair ships, but not on carriers, battleships, destroyers, frigates, submarines or other combat vessels.

Critics: With women aboard, sex and jealousies could create tensions in crews. Pregnancy leaves could leave crucial jobs unfilled. Emergencies require difficult tasks, like carrying pumps down ladders, that almost all women fail in tests. Quarters, especially on subs, have open toilets and no privacy. A big ship sunk could mean hundreds of women killed.

Proponents: Few shipboard jobs require physical strength, and women do most of them on land. Many guns are electronically controlled, and the largest shells are loaded mechanically. Privacy issues have been overcome on supply ships, and even attack submarines could be refitted. Aircraft carriers are huge, and letting women pilots on them, but not mechanics or radar operators, would be absurd. Naval officers who do not go to sea have slim lanes for career advancement. Female officers now serve and fly only on the Lexington, a training carrier, and on logistics ships. Women serve on combat ships in the British and Canadian navies.

Infantry

Women are not allowed in the infantry or paratroops, or in assault and reconnaissance units like Ranger battalions, or in commando units like the Special Forces, Navy SEALs and Delta Force.

Critics: Infantrymen have to fight in mountains, deserts and swamps carrying up to 110 pounds of food, water, radios, mortars, machine guns, grenades, mines, wire, and sometimes wounded friends. U.S. physical training is "gender-normed" to allow for women's lower strength and endurance; combat is not. Weak or slow members may get a whole team killed. Brutal close combat is psychologically devastating, and combat hand-to-hand is won largely by strength. Women would destroy unit "bonding" and weaken fighting power. Men would go easy or take risks for them. Few enlisted women want transfers to combat units, and might quit instead.

Proponents: Some women can pass infantry training—tests suggest that the strongest 20% of women are as strong as the weakest 20% of men—and want to fight. They already face death or capture in transport, communications, intelligence, military police and medical units. Modern soldiers ride armored personnel carriers or helicopters to battle more often than they march. It is hard for women officers to aspire to top ranks without Ranger school and combat service. Women "bond" with units in guerrilla armies. Taking risks for team members is called heroism.

Armor

Women may not serve in the tanks, armored personnel carriers, self-propelled howitzers and mobile anti-aircraft that spearhead ground assaults.

Critics: Crews may have to get out surrounded by enemy infantry and fight. Loaders must load three 50-pound shells in 10 seconds, and every crew member must be able to do every job. Tanks must be repaired in the field, and even the track wrenches weigh 68 pounds. There is no privacy in a tank.

Proponents: Tank jobs do not involve as much lifting or endurance as the infantry.

Artillery

Women are excluded from field artillery, which fires at targets nearby and up to about 20 miles way. They are in long-range and air-defense artillery, firing Patriot missiles, for example.

Critics: Gun crews must be able to load ten 45-pound shells or four 100-pound shells a minute, and pack and move in a hurry. Artillery positions get attacked.

Proponents: Artillery is on treads or moved by trucks. Gun crews divide the heavy work. Units rarely fight hand-to-hand unless they are overrun, and women are already expected to fight if that happens.

Engineers

Women may not be combat engineers, who clear minefields, cut razor wire, explode obstacles, create landing strips, dig gun emplacements, string wire, lay minefields and the like.

Critics: Engineers often lead the way for attacking infantry and meet heavy combat. Heavy physical labor is part of the job.

Proponents: Women drive heavy machinery and do construction work as civilians.

WOMEN IN THE WILD BLUE YONDER[5]

Now that Congress has opened the door for women to enter the ranks of combat pilots, many Americans find themselves uncomfortable with the idea. Why do so many people cringe at the thought of women in combat? Full access to the military is a logical next step on the road to equal opportunity for women. Perhaps the real question is why it has taken so long for women to enter battle.

The combat barrier somehow seems different, more ominous than other rights gained by women. Not because it marks the invasion of women into one of the few remaining bastions of masculinity, but because it threatens what is perhaps the sole surviving gender myth of the 20th century: that women are the world's nurturers. Can a nurturer also be a destroyer?

Those opposed to sending women into combat sidestep the issue. Some claim that women are not physically strong enough to

[5]Article by Elaine Tyler May, author of "Homeward Bound: American Families in the Cold War Era" and teacher of history at the University of Minnesota. From *The New York Times*, Ag 8, 1991. Copyright 1991, *The New York Times*. Distributed by *The New York Times* Special Features. Reprinted with permission.

serve as fighter pilots. That argument collapses at a time when strength and endurance are as readily developed in women as in men. Besides, these women would be flying planes, not lifting them. And with sophisticated weaponry, women can push the buttons to drop the bombs as easily as men can.

Others argue that men should protect women, not the other way around. That chivalry might make some sense if it operated anywhere else in our society. But women are at risk in other occupations, where hazards to their safety abound. It is disingenuous to hear calls for their protection in battle when they are not even protected at home, where domestic abuse and violence against women are widespread.

Still maybe war is different. Since our War of Independence, women have participated in warfare. They have provided supplies and medical care, even on the front lines. During World War I, men were urged to fight for mothers, wives and sweethearts back home.

In World War II, sentimental views of women were replaced by other images. Rosie the Riveter became a national icon, doing "men's work" in war industries. These female workers were glorified, though they were expected to relinquish their well-paying, physically demanding jobs after the war. At the same time, symbols of female sexuality entered the iconography of war. Pinups appeared in military barracks; the noses of thousands of bombers were decorated with erotic portraits.

If the U.S. hires women as professional killers, allowing them into the cockpit, what remains of the sentimental ideal of women as pure and gentle creatures might vanish. It is not so much that women might get killed; it is that they might kill.

The ability to kill is the ultimate equalizer. Indeed, the integration of combat units after World War II signaled a major change in the nation's racial relations. The symbolic impact of women fighting in combat cannot be overlooked.

Power, of course, is intimately connected to sex. It is no accident that another policy under discussion bans homosexuals from the armed forces. In World War II and the cold war, women and gays were barred from combat, in part because they were believed to be security risks.

We now know that in spite of the ban, many gay men and women served heroically in World War II. Still, military policies are based on the theory that the only good fighting force is one in which heterosexual men pursue their mission free from sexual temptation. Since no such force has ever existed, it is difficult to know if there is any truth to the myth.

There are those on the other side of the debate who argue that women are really less warlike than men and that bringing them fully into the military would humanize the armed services. Perhaps. But we won't know, at least not until women fill the leadership ranks of the military establishment—from running major defense industries and the Pentagon to serving as the Commander in Chief herself.

WOMEN WARRIORS?: EQUALITY, YES—MILITARISM, NO[6]

What had been unthinkable twenty years ago and unattainable ten years ago—the full integration of women into the voluntary service—is now on the horizon. On July 31 [1991], the Senate struck a blow for women's equality in the armed services when it voted to eliminate regulations that prohibited women in the Air Force and Navy from flying combat missions. The House had done the same in May. The forces fighting for women's equal opportunity seem to have scored a major, if mostly symbolic, victory at a time when women's rights are being sledgehammered by state legislatures, the courts and the Bush Administration. It's a victory, that is, if you consider elimination of combat exclusions an unadulterated feminist achievement.

In 1980, feminists of various stripes publicly wrestled with the question of women's relationship to the military. A case before the Supreme Court, *Rostker v. Goldberg*, filed by a men's veterans group, challenged the constitutionality of a male-only draft. *Rostker* was championed by the National Organization for Women. NOW and its president at the time, Eleanor Smeal, were criticized by many peace activists and antimilitarist feminists for their stance.

This time around, NOW is still advocating the equal opportunity position on women and the military, as are many other na-

[6]Article by Annette Fuentes, from *The Nation* magazine; O 28, 1991, 253:516+.

tional women's legal and policy organizations. But the voices of feminists who consider combat inclusion a dubious advance have been muted. The sole debate has been between conservative types who think G.I. Jane will sabotage male bonding on the frontlines, and the equal rights advocates who argue that dropping all barriers to women in the military is not only fair, it contributes to military preparedness.

"The only thing exclusion protects is men's jobs," said Patricia Ireland, executive vice president of NOW. "It limits the services' ability to put the best people in the jobs." When pressed, she acknowledged NOW's pacifist philosophy, but said that "women need to be in all the powerful institutions in society. As long as the military and Congress remain men's clubs, women's perspective is excluded and public policy is worse for it."

The gulf war provided the main impetus to Congress's action. "Obviously, as a result of Operation Desert Storm, attention has been focused on the 1948 laws restricting women in the military," says Carolyn Becraft, a former Army officer who works for Women's Research and Education Institute. "The gulf war showed women in combat." Indeed, the 35,000 women deployed in the Persian Gulf were front and center in press coverage of that military action. Eleven women died in the war, five in combat. Two women were taken prisoner. Who could deny that women had proved their mettle and deserved all the opportunities men get in the armed forces?

Certainly not the U.S. public. A *Newsweek* poll taken during the war found that 63 percent of respondents approved of having women pilots, 53 percent said women should have combat assignments if they want them and 50 percent believed any future draft should include women. The Pentagon has been testing the waters of public opinion regarding women in combat situations since the 1983 invasion of Grenada. Press censorship in that operation was so impenetrable that no images of the 170 women soldiers sent to the island leaked out.

Panama was next, and the public got a closer look at 800 women who were getting a closer look at combat. Still, the military was sensitive to coverage of their participation. One wire story reported that two women drivers refused to ferry troops into Panama City during heavy fighting. But, in an expert display of damage control, public affairs officers exonerated the drivers in a statement that was attached to a release about two female helicopter pilots who received medals of valor.

By contrast, the coverage of Desert Storm was a red, white, and blue tribute to women soldiers. When a Scud missile destroyed a U.S. barracks in Saudi Arabia, killing twenty-eight, including two women, it also seemed to smash old definitions of frontline and combat zones. Predictions that Americans couldn't tolerate women coming home in body bags were exploded, too. A majority of them apparently don't care about keeping women out of harm's way anymore.

From the Pentagon's perspective, the use of women the services is "a labor issue," says Linda De Pauw, a historian and founder of The Minerva Center on women and the military in Arlington, Virginia. "What's driving the extended use of women is military need, especially in the modern army. Military work has become increasingly technological." Expanding the role of the growing number of female soldiers "fits in with the idea of Workforce 2000 [the Hudson Institute's phrase for the work force of the future], which is increasingly women and minority," she says. "Smart managers see they can't be bigots. It's counterproductive."

In fact, women of color make up 38 percent of all women (officers and enlisted) in the services; black women alone are 30 percent. In the Army, women of color are 55 percent of all enlisted women; black women are 47 percent. "The military has always provided equal opportunity. In that way, it is way ahead of the civilian sector," says Becraft. The retention of black women is very high, she says, because they have fewer opportunities in civilian life than black men.

Nonetheless, women of color aren't getting their fair share of the best jobs and highest ranks. Minority women are 41 percent of all enlisted women, yet only 19 percent of women officers. Statistics on the U.S. Army in Europe reveal that women of color occupy 50 percent of the lowest-ranking and lowest-paid jobs in the military. In Germany, for example, they are 51 percent of all women soldiers and 3.5 percent of officers; three times as many white women are officers.

Rank is a primary factor in the discussions of combat restrictions. The women pilots who want access to combat missions are officers whose promotions and career paths are blocked without combat-related jobs. Just 324 women pilots in the Air Force and 248 in the Navy would immediately benefit from the legislative changes. The remaining statutory obstacles to women entering combat assignments are in the Navy and Marine Corps, which prohibit women from serving on ships on combat missions. In the Army, policy, not law, bars women from jobs considered to involve direct combat.

So the fight to end combat exclusions is driven from above. "It's absolutely true that officers are more supportive of repealing combat exclusions than enlisted," says Becraft. "Enlisted women are like blue-collar workers in their career progression. I don't think they want to be in the infantry." And who can blame them? A person might see the movie *Top Gun* and want to fly like Tom Cruise. But has anyone walked out of *Platoon* and signed up to be a grunt?

Although existing physical standards would exclude most women from ground combat roles should the Army change its policies, Phyllis Schlafly and other conservatives have harped on the image of women in muddy trenches to fire up the debate. The temptation to rebut their views and the choicest sexist statements emanating from old-timers at the Pentagon is certainly great. In June Gen. Robert Barrow told a Senate subcommittee addressing women and combat that "I may be old-fashioned, but I think the very nature of women disqualifies them from doing it. Women give life, sustain life, nurture life. They do not take it."

There was a time when feminists would make the very same argument and challenge the very existence of the military as well. But "women's groups have been dealing with multicultural and multiracial organizing," says Sara Lee Hamilton, director of the Nationwide Women's Program of the American Friends Service Committee. "There's been less energy in the movement left over to oppose militarism." Without a broader context into which to place the issue, some feminists have decided to go mano-a-mano with the boys, duking it out on their turf. "I see the issue of repealing combat exclusions as commensurate with improving military readiness," says Michele Beneke, a former air defense officer and legal intern for the American Civil Liberties Union who was liaison to the Gay and Lesbian Military Freedom Project. "I also see it as a citizenship issue. In American society, military service is a hallmark of citizenship. Women won't be full citizens until they can serve in any [every] capacity in the military." Proponents of this position say you've got to separate the nasty things the U.S. military actually does from its role as public employer. "You can be against the way the military is used and still say the structure should work with equal opportunity," says De Pauw. "The apparatus of the military is neutral. You can use the hierarchical organization for different things. The planet needs a lot of work. We could use armies to clean up toxic wastes."

Considering that the military is responsible for some of the worst toxic waste sites, such an idea is ironic to Cynthia Enloe, Clark University professor of government and author of *Bananas, Beaches and Bases*. Enloe says, "What gets left out of the discussion is the very issue of militarism. The way the military is discussed makes it look like *General Hospital*. I'm dismayed that NOW hasn't articulated a position around militarism."

"If it took this long to get women into combat, how long will it take to get everyone out?" asks theologian Mary Hunt, co-director of the Women's Alliance for Theology, Ethics and Ritual in Silver Spring, Maryland. "The issue is to be able to name those advances for women that aren't really feminist. Is the nomination of Judge Clarence Thomas really a civil rights achievement?" Hunt sees the issue of equal opportunity in the military as an example of what progressives face in the 1990s. "We're seeing cosmetic solutions, not substantive change. The advances are really retreats. And it requires the complicity of groups who seek to improve the lot of their members."

Advocates of women in the military frequently draw an analogy to black history and civil rights struggles. Black men faced barriers to integration just as women do today, they say, and there is less racism in the services than in the civilian world. "African-Americans seek heroes. Even people who think we shouldn't have been in the Persian Gulf look at Colin Powell with awe," says Barbara Omolade, counselor at the Center for Worker Education at the City College in New York. "People have always said black people can't fight. So we join the Army to prove it. That same thrust has picked up around women. But blacks have not found true equality through military service. And having Powell at the top won't change foreign policy."

One pillar of the equal-opportunity argument is the concept of the "new, improved Army": one that does good deeds, like delivering humanitarian aid to the Kurds. Forget that the U.S. Army helped make them refugees in the first place. It's the military of a new generation of men and women developing "a new type of relationship . . . a nurturing relationship based upon respect, based on sharing the same hardships," in the words of Carol Barkalow, an Army captain and author of *In the Men's House*. Becraft says it's a less hierarchical military in which "young people have more similar value systems, are more willing to value difference—a multicultural work force."

This touchy-feely rhetoric implies that women soldiers will humanize a brutal male domain. Today's soldiers, like the Teenage Mutant Ninja Turtles of cartoon fame, will become warriors for peace. Of course, the idea of a downsized U.S. military as peacekeeping force goes hand-in-glove with the demise of the cold war's enormous standing Army. But if the Pentagon is selling the notion that its mission is changing, we don't have to buy it. "Do you call Grenada, Panama and the gulf war 'peacekeeping'?" asks Hunt.

Separating equal opportunity from military might is difficult for feminists with a global perspective. Can we be proud that a woman pilot might in the future strafe fleeing Iraqi women and children on a mop-up mission? Enloe is concerned that the only position on women, combat and the military being articulated is the equal-opportunity view. "The worrisome narrowness of the debate and the silence of U.S. antimilitarist feminists have a powerful effect [on] other countries." She says that, thanks to Cable News Network, U.S. women soldiers were a major story in NATO countries like Italy, Canada, Britain and Germany, where the issue of women and combat is a salient one. Italian women, who cannot join the military, will hold a conference in November, says Enloe. "They're trying to figure out what Italian feminists should be thinking about militarism."

The current House-Senate negotiations on their bills to remove combat restrictions for women pilots offer another opportunity to examine the issue. Barriers to advancement for women who choose a military career should and probably will be dropped. Perhaps that will be the bone Congress tosses to women, instead of securing abortion rights and restoring welfare cuts.

But those whose vision of feminism extends beyond career trajectories to the search for wholeness inextricably tied to justice need to say there is another perspective on citizenship, valor and patriotism. A first-class female citizenship is founded on serving people, not destructive foreign policies. Let's not get so tangled up in yellow ribbons that we forget the connection between the battles women wage domestically to feed themselves and their families and a ravenous military machinery that swallows nations whole.

ARMY WOMEN[7]

At 0055 hours on December 20, 1989, U.S. Army helicopters lifted off from Howard Air Force Base, in Panama, to carry infantry across the Panama Canal. Their mission was to assault Fort Amador, one of the few strongholds of the Panamanian Defense Forces to offer resistance to the American forces that had invaded Panama as part of Operation Just Cause. Two of the helicopter pilots ferrying the troops were women: First Lieutenant Lisa Kutschera and Warrant Officer Debra Mann. Their Black Hawk helicopters, officially designated transport, not attack, aircraft, carried troops into what turned out to be "hot" areas, where the PDF was firing on helicopters. For their participation in the assault Kutschera and Mann (and their male counterparts) would be awarded Air Medals—a much coveted decoration.

At about the same time Kutschera and Mann were doing their jobs in the air, Captain Linda Bray, the commander of the 988th Military Police Company was directing her unit to seize a Panamanian military dog kennel. Initial press reports stated that Captain Bray led a force of soldiers in a full-blown fire fight resulting in the deaths of three Panamanian soldiers. In fact no human casualties were suffered and what actually happened remains murky to this day. Still, the incident came to be portrayed as the first time a woman had led U.S. troops into combat.

One other incident involving women soldiers in Panama also attracted attention. Press reports of female cowardice centered on two women truck drivers who allegedly refused orders to drive troops into areas where Panamanian snipers were active. A subsequent account put forth by the Army was quite different. After eight straight hours of driving during the invasion, the two drivers became concerned about whether they could continue to drive their vehicles safely. Tears were shed at some point. Fresh

[7]Article by Charles Moskos, from *The Atlantic Monthly*, Ag. 1990, 266:70-4+.

drivers replaced the two women. A subsequent investigation concluded that at no time was anyone derelict in her duty, and the incident was closed without disciplinary action.

All told, some 800 female soldiers participated in the invasion of Panama, out of a total of 18,400 soldiers involved in the operation. Probably about 150 of the women were in the immediate vicinity of enemy fire. Owing to the publicity that women performing hazardous duty attracted, the once-dormant issue of the ban on women in combat units suddenly came awake.

Title 10 of the U.S. Code precludes women from serving aboard combat vessels or aircraft. Although there are actually no statutory restrictions on how army women can be deployed, the Army derived its combat-exclusion policy from Title 10 and prohibits women from joining direct combat units in the infantry, armor forces, cannon-artillery forces, and combat engineers. The Army's formal definition reads as follows: "Direct combat is engaging an enemy with individual or crew-served weapons while being exposed to direct enemy fire, a high probability of direct physical contact with the enemy's personnel, and a substantial risk of capture."

Although many obstacles to women's participation in the military have been overcome, the line that excludes women from combat units has not yet been crossed. None of the women who participated in the Panama invasion, even those who came in harm's way, were assigned to combat units. Rather, they were serving as military police, medical and administrative staff, and members of transportation, communications, maintenance, and other support units.

The issue of women in combat highlights the dramatic recent changes in the role of women in the military. Visitors at most military installations today will see women in numbers and roles unthinkable at the time the Vietnam War ended. Some 230,000 women now make up about 11 percent of all military personnel on active duty. Each branch of the military has a distinctive history with respect to women. The Air Force, which is 14 percent female, has the highest proportion of jobs open to women, mainly because none of its ground jobs involve combat. Although women are precluded from piloting bombers and fighter planes, they fly transport planes and serve on the crews of refueling planes, such as those that took part in the 1986 U.S. raid on Libya. The

Navy, which is 10 percent female, did not allow women on ships other than hospital ships until 1977, but today women sailors serve aboard transport and supply ships. The Marine Corps is only five percent female, because a high proportion of its members serve in the combat arms. The Army, which is 11 percent female, has the largest total number of women (86,000), and is the vanguard service insofar as the role of women is concerned.

My research as a military sociologist has allowed me to observe at close hand the changing face of the Army since my days as a draftee, in the late 1950s. The account that follows, which briefly surveys the life, the sentiments, and the aspirations of women in the U.S. Army, draws upon my observations of Army units around the world but is based mainly on interviews with soldiers of every rank who participated in the invasion of Panama, including most of the women soldiers who were closest to the shooting.

Some Background

When the second world war broke out, the only women in the armed services were nurses. But manpower needs caused the precursor to the Women's Army Corps (WAC) to be established in May of 1942, followed shortly thereafter by the Navy's WAVES (Women Accepted for Voluntary Emergency Service) and the Coast Guard's SPARs (from "*Semper Paratus*: Always Ready"). Women were allowed into the Marine Corps in 1943, and, refreshingly, these volunteers were called simply Women Marines. Some 800 civilian women who served as Air Force service pilots flew military aircraft across the Atlantic. The Women in the Air Force (WAF) was created in 1948, after the Air Force had become a separate service.

The Women's Armed Services Integration Act of 1948 gave permanent status to military women, but with the proviso that there would be a two-percent ceiling on the proportion of women in the services (excluding nurses). No female generals or admirals were to be permitted. For the next two decades women averaged only a little over one percent of the armed forces, and nearly all of them did "traditional" women's work, in health-care and clerical jobs. During the Vietnam War some 7,500 women served in Vietnam, mostly in the Army. The names of eight women are engraved on the Vietnam Veterans Memorial, in Washington, D.C.

Starting in the 1970s a series of barriers fell in relatively rapid succession. On June 11, 1970, women were promoted to the rank of general for the first time in U.S. history. The new generals were Anna Mae Hayes, of the Army Nurse Corps, and Elizabeth P. Hoisington, the director of the WACs. Women first entered the Reserve Officer Training Corps on civilian college campuses in 1972. Much more traumatic was the admission in 1976 of the first female cadets into the service academies. Today one of seven entrants to West Point is female, although, if truth be told, most of the male cadets are not yet reconciled to the presence of women. Congress abolished the WACs in 1978, leading to the direct assignment of women soldiers to non-combat branches of the Army. Today 86 percent of all military occupational specialties (MOSes) for enlisted personnel are open to women.

To put the combat-exclusion rule into practice and minimize the possibility that women in noncombat MOSes would be assigned to areas where they received hostile fire, the Army in 1983 implemented a system of direct-combat-probability coding (DCPC). The purpose of the probability code is to exclude female soldiers, whatever their MOS, from areas where they are likely to be, to use formal Army terminology, "collocated" with troops in direct combat. But once assigned to an area, Army policy states, female soldiers "in the event of hostilities will remain with their assigned units and continue to perform their assigned duties." This is what happened in Panama with the female helicopter pilots, military police, and truck drivers who came under fire. (In contrast, during the 1983 American invasion of Grenada four military policewomen were sent to the island with their unit only to be sent right back to Fort Bragg because of the fighting on the island.) DCPC is based on a linear concept of warfare, as is clear from the guideline that women soldiers not be assigned to positions found "forward of the brigade rear boundary"—that is, not close to the front lines. The coding is hard to reconcile with checkerboard combat theaters, however. Two of the twenty-three Americans killed in the Panama operation were in noncombat MOSes—a medic and a military policeman— as were thirty-six of the 324 wounded. One of the wounded was a printing and bindery specialist. None of the killed or wounded soldiers were women.

A Glimpse of Daily Life

I flew down to panama shortly after the invasion and, with the Army's permission, talked to scores of soldiers and investigated their living conditions. The enlistment motivations of the men and women I spoke to differed in important respects. For the typical male, economic realities were predominant. Most admitted to having seen few job opportunities in civilian life. The decision to enlist was usually supported by family and friends. For many of the men, joining the Army seemed to be the path of least resistance. The women soldiers were much more likely to have entered the military for noneconomic reasons. They also seemed to be more independent and adventurous than the men. Often they had not received much encouragement from their parents to join the service. Many of the men, and even more of the women, were attracted by the Army's post-service educational benefits. For the women, joining the Army was the result of a decision to "do something different" and get away from a "boring" existence in some backwater community.

Sitting on her bunk in an extremely hot and stuffy room in an old PDF [Panama Defense Force] barracks, one female Private First Class told a not unusual story: "I worked for a while right after high school and then went to a community college. But with working so much, I couldn't be a real student. I quit school and worked as a waitress at a Denny's. I woke up one day and realized I wasn't going anywhere. There had to be more to life than this. I was afraid I would end up marrying some jerk. The Army offered me a GI Bill and a chance to do something different. My mother cried when I told her I was going to join the Army. But I did it anyway and I'm glad. I won't stay in, but I've seen and done a lot more things than my friends back home."

Many of the women had spent time on field maneuvers, living in tents. Since most of the women were assigned to combat-support functions, they were often able to live in large general-purpose tents. Work sections sleep together in one tent during field exercises whenever possible. This is true whether sections are male only or mixed-sex. Women drape blanklets over a rope between the main tent poles to gain some privacy, although someone on the other side can easily peer over the top. In mixed-sex tents the men generally display some regard for privacy, although not always as much as the women would like. Most of the women sleep in gym clothes or their BDUs (battle dress uniforms), as fatigues are now called. Others become acrobats and manage to change clothes inside their sleeping bags. Almost all the women said they would prefer to sleep in a mixed-sex tent with workmates rather than in a female-only tent with strangers.

Personal cleanliness and hygiene are of much greater concern to women than to men in the field. Even under the tense, busy circumstances of Panama, the women tried to bathe once a day. One young female soldier insisted (wrongly) to me that Army regulations guarantee women a shower at least once every three days. How to wash became almost an obsession for women in the field. One method was to post a guard outside a tent and take a "bird bath," using a can of hot water. One unit moved garbage cans inside the tent for the women to use as stand-up bathtubs. When outside shower facilities were all that was available, women often showered in their BDUs. Female soldiers are expected to plan ahead and provide their own sanitary napkins or tampons. In Panama tampons had to be drawn from the medical-supply system rather than the regular quartermaster system. This created problems for some women in the early days of the invasion. But once life began to return to normal, tampons (and women's underwear) could be readily bought at the post exchange. All in all, menstruation did not seem to worry the female soldiers I spoke with, and it was never invoked as an excuse for absence from work.

Sexual harassment is one of the issues most frequently discussed by women in the military. Enlisted women and female officers differ on this matter in important ways. Enlisted women, like most men of any rank, define sexual harassment mainly in terms of sexual propositions and actual touching. One female sergeant put it this way: "Sexual harassment is making unwelcome advances the second time." Enlisted women also tend to see sexual harassment in almost fatalistic terms, something that "goes with the territory" and is often brought on by the behavior of the woman. But they do not consider every advance to be harassment. Fraternization between men and women among enlisted personnel in the Army (and among Army officers) is as common as it is among students at a coeducational college, and is accepted as normal if it occurs among soldiers (or officers) of the same rank. Most women soldiers who have boyfriends have boyfriends who are soldiers, and the women who are married are far more likely to be married to soldiers than married male soldiers are.

Female officers understand sexual harassment in much broader terms, to include sexist remarks, sex-based definitions of suitable work, the combat-exclusion rule, and so on. Women officers see sexism in the military as something that requires constant vigilance. One lieutenant told me that she found it a "welcome challenge to deal with male chauvinists on a daily basis."

Another form of sexual harassment was mentioned by the enlisted women: approaches from lesbians. The true incidence of lesbianism (and of male homosexuality) in the military is unknown. There are indications that lesbianism is more widespread in the armed forces than is male homosexuality. Defense Department statistics, whether they reflect selective prosecution or not, show that women are discharged for lesbianism almost ten times as often, proportionately, as men are discharged for homosexuality. Accounts of lesbianism were offered spontaneously in most of my extended interviews with female soldiers. My general impression was that lesbianism causes much less alarm among women soldiers than homosexuality does among the men. Whereas male soldiers expressed disdain for homosexuals with sardonic humor if not threats of violence, the women were more likely to espouse an attitude of live and let live.

That enlisted women must face being characterized by many men in the military as either loose or lesbian is an unfortunate reality. These attitudes decline markedly when men and women work together over the long term. Such situations also seem eventually to bring out the best in the men. But sex-related issues by no means pervade the everyday existence of female soldiers. The most common topics of concern and conversation, for both sexes, appear to have little to do with sex. They have to do with the work of the Army and with the good and bad of military life.

Sergeants, Officers, and Enlisted Women

The army's noncommissioned officers in habit the middle ground between the enlisted ranks and the officer corps. If women sometimes occupy an ambiguous position within the military, female NCOs occupy the most ambiguous position of all. One reason is that there are not many of them: only four percent of all senior sergeants are women.

One Sergeant First Class I interviewed, a personnel specialist, joined the Army in 1972. She told me, "I wanted to see the world, and I sure have—Korea, Germany, and now Panama. I was glad to see the WACs go. There were too many cliques and too much politics. The real problem now is that the female NCO is never taken as seriously as the male. Every time we are reassigned to a new unit, we have to prove ourselves all over again. Our credentials aren't portable like the men's."

Like many female NCOs, this woman admits to having few close friends in the military. "If you get too close to the men, they think you're having an affair. If you hang around with women, they think you're a lesbian. Let's face it, you can't really be one of the boys. The kind of insults men throw at each other a woman can't do, unless she wants to cross an invisible line of respect." The sergeant finally brought up the matter of marriage, which weighs heavily with female careerists in the Army: "I never married," she said, "because I just couldn't think of having children and making a go of an Army career." Only 60 percent of female senior NCOs are married, and of those only half have children. A military career works powerfully on military women to keep them single and childless.

Above the rank of noncommissioned officers in the Army is the officer corps, where today one lieutenant in six is female—but only one colonel in thirty. Only three of the Army's 407 general officers are women. Women officers feel the same pressures not to marry or raise children that female NCOs do—pressures that male soldiers do not feel. Many women officers believe that the demands of an Army career preclude having children, and they leave the service. Others make the Army a career, deciding to stay childless. A female helicopter pilot told me, "Having no children is the sacrifice I make to keep flying." In 1989 among male senior officers 94 percent were married, and 90 percent of these had children; among female senior officers only 51 percent were married, and only half of these had children.

A small but growing group of junior female officers, however, seems to have devised a form of planned parenthood that can accommodate both family and career. It works like this. First, aim to be a company commander, an important "ticket to be punched" on the way up the promotion ladder. Company commanders are usually captains with six or seven years in service, people in their late twenties. Company command is a high-pressure job, but it is often followed by a slack time, such as an assignment to an ROTC position or a staff job in a headquarters command. Women officers are coming to regard this period as the most opportune to have a child.

Almost all junior officers today are commissioned right after college. This contrasts with the biographies of today's senior women officers, who entered as WACs, often after some work experience. Brigadier General Evelyn "Pat" Foote, who was one of the Army's most senior women officers when she retired, last year, was well known in the military for being an outstanding and confident professional officer who spoke her mind. She joined the Army at age thirty after a string of white-collar jobs in which, she told me, she always seemed to be "somebody's girl Friday." In her nearly three decades in the Army, Foote served as the commander of a WAC company, as a public-affairs officer in Vietnam, as a faculty member at the Army War College, and as the commander of the Military Police Group in Mannheim, West Germany. She concluded her career as the commanding general of Fort Belvoir, Virginia. She has never married.

Foote espouses a philosophy that is embraced by most senior women officers, at least in private. They hope for a future that harks back to an era when women soldiers, in the main, were unmarried, had no children and few outside distractions, and were more committed to military service than their male counterparts. By now, of course, this is simply too much to expect of female career soldiers.

Foote recognizes that many Army women have been able to combine a military career, marriage, and children. She is adamant that there is little place in the Army for single pregnant women and single mothers. Certainly having pregnant soldiers in deployable units is "the height of folly." In 1988 eight percent of the total female enlisted force bore children; some 15 percent of all enlisted Army women are single parents. Before 1975 pregnant women were routinely discharged from the Army. Today, although pregnant women are ineligible for enlistment, they can remain in the Army if already enlisted. No one knows for sure, but informed sources believe that about a third of pregnant soldiers elect to have their babies and stay in the Army; the women are granted a six-week maternity leave. Another third have abortions and remain in the Army. The remainder leave the service after delivery.

Foote would "feel comfortable" with a rule that expelled pregnant women but allowed waivers on a case-by-case basis. She also notes the problem of pregnant women who carry on too long with their duties to the detriment of themselves and their babies. Single parents too often present "an untenable mess," Foote says. "Anyone, male or female, who can't perform their mission has no place in the Army." She ruefully notes that female officers were never consulted on the changes that allowed pregnant women and single parents to remain in the Army. The "male hierarchy caved in to so-called liberals without thinking what this would mean for Army readiness."

What About Combat?

The various arguments for and against women in combat are complex, and the issues involved are not subject to easy empirical resolution. Whether the propensity of most males to be more aggressive than most females is due mainly to body chemistry or to cultural conditioning is a matter of controversy; so is whether male bonding is chemical or cultural. There are social realities that need be considered, however. We should not forget, for example, that combat troops live, bathe, and sleep together for days and weeks on end. No institution in American society forces men and women into such unrelentingly close contact. That women could be killed or captured in war is a specter raised by those who oppose letting women into combat units. Is this really an issue? Female police officers have died in the line of duty without raising any particular outcry. On the touchy matter of prisoners of war, we have seen at least a symbolic change. In 1988 President Ronald Reagan signed an executive order revising the Code of Conduct for POWs. What formerly began with "I am an American fighting man" was changed to the gender-neutral and less bellicose "I am an American."

What we do know a lot about are differences between the sexes in physical strength and endurance. Statistically speaking, average female upper-body strength is 42 percent less than average male upper-body strength. Looked at another way, the statistics mean that on the average the top fifth of women in lifting capacity are the equal of the bottom fifth of men on the same measure. This means that any work requiring heavy lifting or carrying a great deal of weight—the burden of the combat soldier—puts women at a serious disadvantage. Opponents of the combat-exclusion rule point out that much of modern warfare is technological and "push-button" and does not require the brute strength of the combat soldier of old. There is some truth to this. But women are already allowed in almost all areas of technological warfare, including holding the launching keys of nuclear missiles. The irreducible fact remains that physical strength and endurance are still the hallmarks of the effective combat soldier on the ground; indeed, such qualities may be more important in the future, when we make use of rapid-deployment forces, whose members must carry most of their equipment on their backs.

Experience from foreign countries is not very enlightening on the matter of women in combat. Contrary to popular belief, women in Israel, which is the only country with a female draft, are not assigned to duty as combat soldiers; they played only a limited, mainly defensive, role in the War of Independence, in 1948. A ruling by Canada's Human Rights Commission last year held that women could no longer be excluded from any military role except in submarines. The Canadian experience has not been heartening for those who seek to end the combat-exclusion rule in this country. Only seventy-nine women were recruited into the infantry training program and only one completed the course. She has since requested a transfer out of the infantry.

For all this, it is probably the case that most senior female officers privately second the views of General Foote on the subject of women and combat. Foote favors opening all roles to women in the Army, even in the combat arms. Being a woman per se should not, she says, be a disqualification for any military job. Of course, Foote recognizes the differences in strength between men and women. She acknowledges that few women belong in the infantry, and probably not many more belong in the armor or artillery, but says that certainly some could perform well in those roles, and there is no good reason to exclude women from combat aviation. Her basic position is this: "Never compromise standards. Be sure that anybody in any MOS can do everything required in that MOS."

The problem with the combat-exclusion rule, Foote argues, is that it "develops a whole male cadre and officer corps that doesn't know how to work with women." So long as officers in the combat branches are practicing "a different sheet of music," she says, they will not know how to use women to their full capabilities. At the very least the direct-combat-probability code—"the most counterproductive policy in the U.S. Army"—ought to be abolished, she says, because it prevents trained and qualified women from performing their assignments where they are needed.

How female officers and enlisted personnel variously gauge their future Army career opportunities makes for differing views on women in combat. Female officers see their career opportunities as diminishing as they become more senior. Without a chance for command assignments in combat units, the women officers believe, their careers are limited, especially by comparison with men's careers. Although a government study released last year showed that women are promoted at a rate similar to that for men, the fact remains that the combat-exclusion rule precludes any significant number of women from becoming generals, or even full colonels. Among the female officers I talked with in Panama, about three quarters believed that qualified women should be allowed to volunteer for combat units and about a quarter said that women should be compelled to enter combat units, just as men are. A female military-police officer expressed the sentiments of most: "If a woman has the capability and gumption to enter a combat unit, I'd say go for it. Few of us could make it in the infantry. God forbid that the Army shoehorn women into the infantry to meet some kind of quota. But a woman is as brave as a man, and we shouldn't be kept out of jobs we could do, no matter what the danger. Military women are their own worst enemy by accepting a lowering of physical standards. If we kept standards up, if we kept pregnant women out, then any woman in any MOS would be assigned wherever she was needed when the balloon goes up."

Enlisted women, on the other hand, are less subject to career disappointment, because their expectations are not high to begin with. Inasmuch as they generally did not see themselves in long-term Army roles, the women I spoke with thought of their service in Panama as a one-time-only adventure. Enlisted women foresaw their eventual life's meaning in family, in work outside the military, or, if in the military, in relatively sedentary and routine jobs. Among the enlisted women I interviewed in Panama, about three quarters said that women should not be allowed in combat units and about a quarter said that women who were physically qualified should be allowed to volunteer for combat roles. None of the enlisted women favored forcing women into combat assignments. One female driver gave a typical enlisted woman's response: "I'm old-fashioned. I want to be treated like a woman. I don't want people to think I'm a man. I certainly wouldn't want to be in the infantry. A normal woman can't carry a rucksack that the guys can. Even if we could, the guys would hate us for being there. And, let's face it, we would probably make things harder on everybody all around. No way."

There is one area where the combat-exclusion rule is questioned by most women and some men: piloting helicopters. The skills required to fly a utility helicopter to transport soldiers into hot zones are not really all that different from those required on gunships such as Cobras and Apaches. In Panama the skills of the female pilots were acknowledged by all to be at least the equal of those of the male pilots. Even the British high command, that most traditional of general staffs, is studying the possibility of allowing women to train as pilots for Harriers, the jump-jet fighters that saw so much action in the Falklands War. Were women to be assigned to U.S. gunships in future hostilities, however, they would almost surely suffer casualties. Even in the small, short war in Panama four helicopters were shot down and many more were hit by enemy fire.

Two things came out loud and clear in my Panama interviews. One is that the worst thing for a woman officer is to be removed from an assignment she has trained for simply because there is danger. A helicopter pilot told me how she felt on invasion day when she was denied a flight assignment that she thought was her due: "I was insane with anger. After nine years of training they left me out. It was the ultimate slam." The second point is that not a single woman, officer or enlisted, said that she would volunteer to be an infantry rifleman. Surely, somewhere in the U.S. Army, there are women who would volunteer for the infantry. But they were not in Panama.

The Unasked Question

Women in the military have been a troublesome issue for feminists. Feminists have also been troublesome for women in the military. Most feminists clearly want women to share equally the rights and burdens of service, but many of them abhor the combat role of the military profession and much of the basic direction of American foreign policy, which the military profession serves. That many of those who opposed the Panama invasion also advocate combat roles for women is indeed ironic. Female officers are understandably distrustful of much of the civilian feminist agenda, with its not-so-veiled anti-military content. Even as they chart new ground in opportunities for women, female officers are unquestionably less liberal politically, on average, than their civilian counterparts.

Where mainstream feminists and senior women officers come together is in their wish to do away with, or at least punch holes in, the categorical exclusion of women from direct combat roles. They see the exclusion as somehow precluding women from full citizenship. Following the Panama invasion and the reports of women in combat, the push to remove the last barriers to women's full participation in the military gained new momentum. Representative Patricia Schroeder, a senior Democrat on the House Armed Services Committee, proposed legislation to set up a trial program to test the suitability of women for the combat arms. Such a program had been recommended in 1989 by the Defense Advisory Committee on Women in the Services. Last April the Army announced that it would not initiate such a trial program. But the Army's decision will not put the issue to rest. As long as there are women in the military, the pressures to end the combat-exclusion rule will remain.

On the surface, the proposal for a trial program sounds eminently reasonable. How can we know whether women will measure up to the stresses of combat without assigning them to combat training and seeing what happens? Admittedly, training is not the same as actual combat, but a pilot program would tell us more than we know now.

There is another matter to consider, however. Let us assume that the presence of women in combat units can be shown not to affect adversely the combat performance of the men in those units. Let us also assume that in the event of hostilities the death of female soldiers would not cause much more upset at home than the death of male soldiers. And let us assume that a pilot program will be established and that it will show some number of women to have the physical and psychological endurance to perform well in combat, or at least as well as some men already in combat roles. Given all this, the pressure to remove the ban on women in combat units will be difficult to resist. But will allowing qualified women to enter the combat arms finally mean the resolution of this nettlesome issue?

Unfortunately, no. The issue is not simply "opening up" combat assignments to military women. The core question—the one avoided in public debate, but the one that the women soldiers I spoke with in Panama were all too aware of—is this: Should every woman soldier be made to confront exactly the same combat liabilities as every man? All male soldiers can, if need arises, be assigned to the combat arms, whatever their normal postings. True equality would mean that women soldiers would incur the same liability. To allow women but not men the option of entering or not entering the combat arms would—rightly or wrongly—cause immense resentment among male soldiers; in a single stroke it would diminish the status and respect that female soldiers have achieved. To allow both sexes to choose whether or not to go into combat would be the end of an effective military force. Honesty requires that supporters of lifting the ban on women in combat state openly that they want to put all female soldiers at the same combat risk as all male soldiers—or that they don't.

A trial program of women in combat roles which shows that women can hold their own in battle may put one argument to rest. But it will signal the start of another.

RIGHT BEHIND YOU, SCARLETT![8]

"Ya gotta have 'em for fighting."

It was Mother's Day, and the San Diego cabbie crushed an empty Sprite can and filed it in his litter bag instead of chucking it onto Interstate 805. "Balls, I mean. That's where the testosterone comes from. No testosterone, no aggression." To the antenna of his Chevy was tied a yellow ribbon.

His fare, an Israeli enjoying a break from the Holy Land, made noises of agreement to be nice. He was wondering how this American had gone all his life without meeting an aggressive

[8]Article by Edward Norden, from *The American Spectator*, Ag. 1991, p. 14-16. ©1991, Edward Norden. Reprinted with permission.

woman—was this possible in California, land of the future? The Israeli tried to keep an open mind, but nothing proved to him so neatly how far the so-called Gulf War had been from a genuine war than cries he heard to junk the laws barring American women from combat.

The Stars and Stripes were everywhere. From coast to coast, it was a season for victory parades to honor the returning heroes. And heroines—in fact, a big push was on to let women fight, really fight, next time. It wasn't enough that 33,000 of them had been shipped to the Gulf, where they had faithfully spotted artillery, loaded bombs, maintained aircraft, driven trucks, sorted mail. Some women and men now wanted women to have an equal opportunity to be honored not only on the Fourth of July, but also on Memorial Day.

It was a major campaign. The Israeli had heard National Public Radio airing the cons and especially the pros of the matter. *Life* magazine, which he was charmed to see had been resurrected, had come out with a handsome spread, the text of which endorsed women's "right to fight." Said *Life*: "Officially, keeping women out of combat positions is supposed to reduce their chances of being hurt. But if this high-tech war proved anything, it proved that the traditional concept of the combat zone has been blurred." Many "myths" had been "buried in the Arabian sands," according to *Life*, including the notions that: (1) "Women can't perform under pressure," (2) "Mother's shouldn't—and don't want to—go to war," and (3) "The public isn't ready for female POW's or women in body bags." In connection with the last ex-myth, *Life* recalled that two women had been captured by the Iraqis and ten killed (of whom two by enemy fire), yet "the public remained composed." Maybe this was because Americans realized that "the idea that one life is more valuable than another insults both sexes."

Those who expressed reservations about women in combat spoke with forked tongues. "Many women (and men) in the military," *Life* explained, "contend that combat exclusion laws protect women from just one thing: promotions." And, although the time was ripe for abolition, "women in the military fear that no one in Congress will be brave enough to stand up for them." No one? In the *Los Angeles Times*, Rep. Patricia Schroeder (D-Colo.) was all for repeal of the sexist statutes, as were Sens. John

Warner (R-Va.) and John McCain (R-Ariz.). "Women," said McCain in odd English, "have demonstrated again that they can perform any role they are called upon to make." In the meantime, the House Armed Services Committee, voting on the 1992 defense budget, had said that women should be able to volunteer to pilot combat missions. Finally, something called the Defense Advisory Committee on Women in the Services, by a vote of 29–4, had asked Secretary of Defense Dick Cheney to work for repeal in all the services. The Israeli was amazed. It had to do, he suspected, with America's all-volunteer military, with Women's Lib and coed military academies. But what, exactly?

A serious type would have gone to the UCSD [University of California at San Diego] library and read the relevant books. What the Israeli did instead was to have the cabbie drop him off at Jack Murphy Stadium for a San Diego Padres game, where two companies of Marines from Camp Pendleton were being hosted. They sat segregated in the second deck overlooking third base, the Israeli at field level overlooking first. Between one pitch and another they suddenly got to their feet as one person and shouted their hymn, to stormy applause. Were there women among them? No, these Marines were as unisex as the Padres and Expos. Whatever the other services were doing, the leathernecks were keeping women away, maybe by requiring that recruits have their heads shaved as smooth as bowling balls. Golani—the Israeli marines, known affectionately as *ha-hayot* ("the animals")—would have bought their girls with them. Of course, Golani girls only instruct, they don't fight.

The middle-aged Israeli himself was used to being instructed in the arts of war by women. Just before leaving, he had been called up, along with other reservists of his potbellied unit, for a refresher course. The instructors in weapons, radio, atomic/biological/chemical warfare, and first aid had been, as usual, women—no, girls, of nineteen or so. Slim, unwrinkled beauties speaking a clipped monotone, they were teaching men twice their age to cock a .50-caliber machine gun. But young women also train raw recruits in the Israeli Defense Forces (IDF). It wasn't the local feminists who forced the IDF to put girls in these slots. The generals decided on their own, the main idea being to make the IDF more formidable by making more males available for combat. Not that women instructors aren't as savvy and dedicated as men. The ones who volunteer and make the grade are great, and it's said that 18-year-old boys learn faster and perform better under their tuition, since anything a girl can do they must do at least as well, right?

Only the ones with a special fire burning in them—tough chicks, smart and patriotic tomboys—get to be instructors and officers. The rest make coffee, answer the phone, shuffle paper, water the plants, and decorate the bases while they cross out the days until discharge. There are lots of young women in khaki all over Israel at all times, thanks to the fact that the IDF drafts almost all boys and girls as soon as they finish high school: 95 percent of the boys go in, with only the ultra-Orthodox exempted because of an old political deal, and about 60 percent of the girls, the rest being excused if they marry, become pregnant, or declare believably that they have religious objections to a scene where men and women are very casual together. Furthermore, unless they sign up for the corps or the professional army, females serve only two years, after which they do no reserve duty, while males serve three, after which they can expect to find themselves in uniform for a month or two every year until age 52. That said, unless you go along on ambushes with the paratroops, or patrols with the navy, you'll see women everywhere in the IDF.

Some of the smartest and best-looking are attached to inteligence, the medical corps, and general headquarters, all based in the rear (if Israel has a rear). Others wear the badges of the air force, paratroops, Golani, navy, armor, and combat engineers. These are the units that come under fire the most, the units among which one most often sees the blood-red epaulet tabs signifying combat experience. The women sporting red epaulets (there are a few) are an exception that proves the rule, since a woman in the IDF earns them not by being in the gory thick of things, where she isn't sent or even allowed to be, but on the fringes, and then usually by accident.

Take the siege of Beirut in 1982. The Israeli rooting for the Padres remembered how it was when PLO Katyusha rockets began impacting around divisional headquarters several miles from the focus of the fighting. It was unexpected, brief, and very unpleasant, the ambulances wailed and the med-evac copters came and went, but the women radio operators kept their cool and carried on, performing under pressure. They doubtless got their tabs. Also, without a doubt, they were reassigned back behind the

Israeli border after the siege, while the IDF spent three years leaving Lebanon, harassed every step of the way by Palestinian, Shi'ite, and Druse snipers, bombers, and kidnappers who giggled at the distinction between front and rear, combatant and non-combatant.

For, in the crunch, IDF women get treated no differently from civilians, and it doesn't matter whether they're tough officers or gentle secretaries. The law says they have to be evacuated in the event of hostilities. That's exactly what happened in the sudden chaos of the Golan Heights when the Syrians attacked on Yom Kippur 1973. Though some IDF career women grumbled about being snatched out of Lebanon and replaced by men, none complained about being taken out of the way of the Syrian army, nor did anyone in the Israeli feminist movement cry sexism.

Israel has its feminists, from the secular right to the Zionist left to the loony left. They fight the usual fights (equal pay for equal work, limitations on porn, abortion on demand, shelters for battered wives), plus a few special ones arising from the Jewishness of the country (relief from the rabbis who rule on divorce). But getting women into combat isn't on their agenda. This is perhaps because they have so much else on their hands, perhaps because even the peace-niks among them know that the IDF has to be a winner and doubt in their hearts that women and combat make a winning combination, perhaps because they subscribe to the widespread Israeli superstition that the death of a young woman is even more of an insult to nature than that of a young man, and most likely because they know that in Israel the "right to fight" won't remain an abstract one for long.

Forty-three years ago women fought for a while, really fought. Women in the pre-state underground had done everything from broadcasting over clandestine radio stations to smuggling guns and explosives in their blouses to seducing British officers, and in the six months between the U.N.'s partition resolution of 1947 and the day the British left, during which the Arabs and Jews were already at war, some of these women saw combat, including the 4-foot, 10-inch, 90-pound future Dr. Ruth Westheimer, last seen by the vacationing Israeli in a TV ad with Bo Jackson. It was a desperate time, when defeat meant massacre and possibly the end of Jewish history, and anyone who could handle a weapon was put in the line. But as soon as the British departed and the IDF was formed, as soon as the situation became merely dicey, the women were removed from the trenches, never to return. You meet the survivors nowadays mainly in *kibbutzim*, sweet grandmotherly types. If you eat everything on your plate, they'll tell you tales to curl your hair.

The heroism for which IDF women are likely to be celebrated these days is of another kind. Lieutenant Osnat Zahir, "although physically and emotionally exhausted . . . displayed an unprecedented level of sensitivity and commitment," in the words of her citation of valor as a nurse at a casualty clearing station in the Sinai during the Yom Kippur War. Which isn't to say that praise and publicity are reserved for bravery in the Florence Nightingale mode. The army girls who earlier this year helped locate people in the rubble of buildings hit by Scuds and extricated them got good press, as did the navy's female radar operators, sitting on dry land, who spotted approaching terrorist dinghies in time. Women in the IDF are expected and encouraged to provide support in the most generous sense of the term. They're not expected or allowed to do more—that is, kill and be killed—and little Israeli girls growing up today aren't presented with what Americans call "role models" for combat. Although "thirtysomething" and "L.A. Law" are broadcast in Israel, "GI Joe" is not, so Israeli kids don't get to hear the comely helicopter crewperson, weapon blazing, shouting "C'mon!" to Joe, who replies, "Right behind you, Scarlett!"

The Israeli grandmothers with their hair-curling memories appear seldom on TV. In school, the scarce women in the Bible who either killed for their people or commanded them in battle—one thinks of Judith displaying the head of Holofernes and Deborah orchestrating the Battle of Kishon—get no great emphasis either. More famous is Hannah Senesh. Parachuted into Hungary in 1944, she was tortured to death by the Gestapo and has a village named after her. Her poems are continuously in print. But she lived and died in those desperate times, not today.

Israel is a complicated and uncomfortable little country, where most of the time most of the people try their best to live as if their common situation weren't still pretty desperate. This requires forgetting a great deal and keeping women out of the front line, even if it's only a few kilometers away. Although Hannah Senesh's example is studied in the schools, nearer to reality are the stereotypes of children's books, which reflect and explain and justify Israeli routine to young Israelis. In one entitled *Daddy Does Reserve Duty*, which seeks to calm a youngster's distress at the absence of a parent, it's taken for granted that Daddy should be the one going off to play soldier while Mommy tends hearth and home.

The Padres blew their lead and lost the game. The fans and Marines took it peacefully. Waiting for the bus that would transport him back to where he was staying, the Israeli was confronted with one of those public service posters that cannot be ignored. It quoted the State of the Union address of January 19, 1991:

> There is no one more devoted, more committed to the hard work of freedom, than every soldier and sailor, every marine, airman and coastguardsman—every man and woman now serving in the Persian Gulf.

Memory is a queer thing. As soon as he read Bush's words, the Israeli thought of two women in quick succession. The first was the GI from Mississippi who was a member of the Patriot crew flown in to protect Tel Aviv and keep the IDF out of the fighting, and the second was Ahuva. He hadn't thought of Ahuva in years.

Now he saw her in his mind's eye, the friend of a friend, an intelligent, gentle, brave, and altogether devoted creature worth her weight in gold and wearing red tabs on her shoulders. She had made major in the IDF and hit the glass ceiling. It wasn't there to stop women but to stop those without rich combat experience, experience women can't get. Ahuva understood perfectly that the purpose of the IDF is to win wars, but she was torn over the consequences: that men will fight and be promoted all the way to the top while women, even the best and most precious, fall away or get stuck. She wasn't eaten up by ambition, she certainly wasn't power-hungry, yet in her gentle eyes the Israeli hadn't been surprised to see a glint of steel, and when she quit her beloved army after fifteen years of eighteen-hour days to have a child, she was almost as mad as she was sad.

The Israeli wondered what she would now have to say about the American women Scud-busters. Had she been one of those who had brought them champagne and cake? Would she consider them to have been in combat, as *Life* did? He was ready to wager that she wouldn't. Combat isn't a job description but a place—a place where a lot of killing and dying is going on. If the Patriot batteries in Israel and Saudi Arabia had begun to be bombed by the enemy, how long would the women have been kept there? If Operation Desert Storm had been a real war, with thousands or tens of thousands of Americans killed, how many women in body bags would Americans have accepted before losing their composure, before demanding either that all women be evacuated or Baghdad nuked?

These were moot, not rhetorical questions. America wasn't Israel. It was conceivable that all of America's wars to come would be brilliant Nintendo games, or that Arlington National Cemetery would fill up with women and the country would tolerate it in the name of justice. But if the latter were the case—*pace* NPR, *Life*, Rep. Schroeder, Sens. Warner and McCain, and the myth-debunking industry—it was hard to approve of where Americans' ideas of "justice" were leading them, and hard to avoid the conclusion that a country that sends its women into battle out of anything short of desperation isn't worth fighting for.

II. IN WHICH SHE SERVES: CAPABILITIES AND CHALLENGES

EDITOR'S INTRODUCTION

Women have gained the right to perform in many formerly male-dominated arenas and are now attempting to enter another, the combat zone. The articles in this section provide an insight into a woman's right to defend her country in the capacity she is allowed to do so, while also delineating her desire to do more.

The opening article is an excerpt from Maj. Gen. Jeanne Holm's book, *Women in the Military*. It provides an extensive examination of the roles military women played in the Persian Gulf crisis and puts a personal face on many of the participants—those who did their duty, those who were captured by the enemy, those who died. The second article, by Andrea Gross, reprinted from *Ladies Home Journal*, delves into the issue of whether women are "fit—and ready—to fight." Women enlist for many of the same reasons men do, the author suggests, such as patriotism, a desire for adventure, self-fulfillment, and education, but parallels cease when they approach the ladder to that "last treehouse," promotion to higher ranks via combat duty.

The next three articles all appeared in a special issue of *Newsweek*. Barbara Kantrowitz recapitulates the debate with its various proponents and detractors. She states: "There are hawks and doves on both sides of the issue." The second article, by Col. David H. Hackworth entitled "War and the Second Sex," discusses a military woman's capabilities and intelligence while questioning whether equality on the battlefield would hurt U.S. combat readiness and national security. The last article is an interview with Carol Barkalow, a West Point graduate who has commanded an air-defense platoon and a truck company. This interview reveals one woman's reasons for choosing a career in the military and what that commitment means to her.

The next article, by Jeannie Ralston from *Life*, ponders the question of why it took only six weeks to liberate Kuwait while the liberation of the military is still unresolved. Ms. Ralston aims to dispell the myths that "women can't perform under pressure," and that the combat zone is no place for women or mothers. The final article, by Peter Cary and Bruce B. Auster, from *U.S. News & World Report*, deals with other challenges to military women. Although mentioned previously, sexual harassment and job discrimination are discussed specifically in relation to the 1992 Tailhook incident. An historical and sociological perspective reemphasizes how difficult it will be for many of the men of the military, from junior officers to top brass, ever to accept women as equals.

DESERT STORM: WHEN POLICY FACED REALITY[1]

"They did it!" Air Force pilot Capt. Stephanie Wells wrote in her diary on 17 January. "The attack has begun at long last. As I figured, the nervousness of anticipation is gone." Even her attitude had shifted from one of almost despair and resignation at the thought of the United States going to war, to "Go get' em and get this thing over with."

Wells' C-5 transport crew agreed that the anticipation and anxiety of waiting for the war to begin was tougher than being in it. On the sixteenth she wrote "H-hour is past. We are on the ground in Bahrain at 0800 (8:00 A.M.). Hostilities are imminent . . . This is the most scared I've felt on this whole business." During the intelligence briefing before departing for Torrejon, Spain, she felt the adrenaline surge of anticipation. She got all her chemical warfare gear out of the bag and ready. The departure from Bahrain and the flight were uneventful, but the whole crew felt the heightened awareness. Wells thought that before the next mission to Saudi she would buy a handgun even though she hated them. "I can think of some scenarios where I might need it," she wrote.

At 12:50 A.M. (local time) Thursday, 17 January, the first fighter planes roared off the runways of the air base at Dhahran,

[1]Permission to reproduce granted by Presido Press, from the book, *Women in the Military*, by Maj. Gen. Jeanne Holm, USAF. Chapter 26, "The Persian Gulf War," pp. 444-461, Copyright 1992. Reprinted with permission.

Saudi Arabia, and U.S. warships offshore launched cruise missiles at Iraqi targets. Before 3 A.M., radar-evading F-117 Stealth fighters had demolished targets in Baghdad as Americans watched the action live on their TV screens. Operation Desert Shield had become Desert Storm. A somber President told America that the liberation of Kuwait had begun: "No president can easily commit our sons and daughters to war."

More than events in Panama, Desert Storm exposed to the American public the problems and contradictions in DOD and service policies on women vis-à-vis combat, and some of the assumptions underlying them.

During the operation, American military women did just about everything on land, at sea, and in the air except engage in the actual fighting, and even there the line was often blurred. They piloted and crewed planes and helicopters over the battle area, serviced combat jets, and loaded laser-guided bombs on F-117 Stealths for raids on targets in Baghdad. They directed and launched Patriot missiles, drove trucks and heavy equipment, and operated all kinds of high-tech equipment. They manned .55-caliber machine guns, guarded bases from terrorist attack, and ran prisoner of war facilities. They repaired and refueled M1 tanks, Bradley fighting vehicles, and earth-moving equipment. Navy women served on naval replenishment and repair ships, fleet oilers offshore, and at facilities ashore; Coast Guard women were involved in harbor security. Other women commanded brigades, battalions, companies, and platoons that provided support and services to the troops in the field. They staffed medical facilities ashore and afloat to receive, treat, and evacuate casualties.

Women also were directly involved in the war effort at installations all over the world and in the United States, supporting the gigantic airlift, sea-lift, and refueling operations, as well as combat operations launched from bases outside the immediate combat theater. While observing preparations for B-52 strikes launched from England, Sen. John Warner was struck by the extent of women's involvement. "At midnight in England, when the troops were loading B-52s (bombers) in the cold misty rain, you couldn't distinguish the men from the women," he said. "The women were loading and fusing the 500-pound bombs the same as the men."

The ground crews at all these bases, as well as the many thousands of military and civilian personnel stationed at installations scattered around the world and in the United States, were as essential to the overall effort in the Gulf as those actually located in the theater.

Of the U.S. services, the Army deployed by far the largest number of military women to the Gulf. It was also burdened by the most complicated policies on assigning them. For their own protection, Army women were not supposed to serve in the front lines or in direct combat units. However, it was obvious from the beginning that front lines were not what they used to be and noncombat units regularly took casualties. In the Gulf War there were no fixed positions or clear lines in the sand—the "front" changed hourly. Units in the rear areas, where the women were concentrated, were often as exposed to attack as those at the front. Iraqi long-range artillery and especially the surface-to-surface missiles were unisex weapons that did not distinguish between combat and support troops. The men and women under Scud attacks knew they were in combat regardless of what the military called it. Their location in the rear provided little protection to the soldiers of the 14th Quartermaster Detachment when a Scud missile slammed into their barracks near Dhahran, Saudi Arabia, killing twenty-eight of them, including three women.

Army policy excluded women from serving in the direct combat units, namely infantry, armor, and cannon artillery. However, on many occasions during Desert Storm, female soldiers in support units found themselves in the thick of the action. Women assigned to units supporting the mechanized forces, for example, moved forward with the combat units into Kuwait and Iraq, often coming under enemy fire.

Moreover, women were assigned to target and launch Patriot missiles because the Army makes distinctions between *defensive* and *offensive* combat. When they were firing their missiles at incoming Scuds, the soldiers in the Patriot batteries, both male and female, must have thought it was a distinction that made a difference.

The principal source of the confusion within the Army was the Direct Combat Probability Coding (DCPC) system, which unnecessarily complicated the management of military personnel at a time when the Army could least afford it. The system was especially troublesome at the unit level, where commanders struggled to keep pace with the shifting, unpredictable demands of the war by getting the most out of the people they had. Although Army leaders in the Pentagon continued to deny it, numerous reports surfaced through unofficial channels that commanders in the field were regularly ignoring the rules and assigning their people where they were most needed—without regard to gender. "I've got a job to do and I need good people," said a combat support battalion commander. "I don't give a damn whether they're a male or female so long as they know what the hell they're doing. This is no place for screw-ups."

Other reports surfaced that Army unit commanders, to be "on the safe side," often applied their own interpretations of the rules. The commanding officer of an enemy prisoner of war camp (EPOW) in Saudi Arabia, for example, decided on his own to ban his female military police from internal prison guard duties even though they were fully qualified to perform them. Their normal primary guard duties were delegated to the male MPs while the women were relegated to answering telephones, checking IDs, issuing clothing, and delousing prisoners' clothing. One of the reassigned women had worked as a correctional officer at a civilian maximum security facility, where she had dealt with tougher customers than any Iraqi soldier. She had fourteen years of military training for the job she had been sent to the Persian Gulf to do and, like the other women, she was incensed at not being allowed to do her job. Understandably, the men resented having to take up the slack. Worst of all, the camp was short of critical, trained personnel to cope with an enormous influx of Iraqi prisoners.

Later, at the same EPOW camp, a team of five military police had to be sent in at 2 A.M. to help quell a riot. Sgt. Kitty Bussell, a member of the team, was stopped by a Saudi who told her that a woman could not go inside on such a dangerous job. Trained in riot control and armed with an M-16 rifle and pistol, Bussell refused to be turned away. "I'm as good a shot as anybody," she insisted and went in.

Women were not permitted to fly the Army's Apache or other attack helicopters; but female pilots of the 101st Airborne Division's Screaming Eagles flew Black Hawk and Chinook helicopters loaded with supplies and troops fifty miles into Iraq as part of the largest helicopter assault in military history. To the Iraqis, the noncombat helicopters flying over the battlefield were as much targets as any Apache and probably a lot easier to hit.

Maj. Marie Rossi [later killed in action], thirty-two, led her squadron of Chinooks during the first assault. However, she almost didn't go because of confusion over the Army's policy. Before the ground assault, Rossi's commander had informed her that all the female pilots were being replaced by men because of the combat restriction. Rossi asked him if the enlisted women on the crews were also being replaced and was told they were not. Rossi reminded him in strong terms that the same policies applied to both officers and enlisted women. He backed down.

There was confusion in the Marine Corps as well. As in the Army, Corps policy banned female leathernecks from all combat jobs and units. Its women were concentrated in the support and combat support units, which normally would have been positioned in the rear areas.

When orders first came to deploy to the Middle East, only the male Marines were shipped out; the female Marines in the same units were left behind. Five days later the female Marines were deployed, but they were annoyed that the Corps could not seem to clarify its policy. The women felt that it was demeaning to them and bred resentment among the men. "It was always my plan to bring the women from day one," the Commanding General explained defensively.

After the women arrived in Saudi Arabia, they were quartered for a time abroad air-conditioned ships while the men were sweltering in tents and warehouses ashore. The men resented the special treatment the women seemed to be getting, and the women resented being treated differently. "We are Marines," complained S. Sgt. Martha Brown, a radio repairman. "We should be treated as Marines." As the Marines settled into their positions in preparation for the ground assault, the double standard disappeared.

Then, in what was described as a "calculated risk," a huge Marine support base was set up well forward of most infantry units and nearest the border of Iraqi-occupied Kuwait. Its mission was to provide logistical support for two infantry divisions. Thus, more than 170 "noncombatant" female Marines assigned to the 2nd Forward Marine Support Group were located in one of the most forward and exposed positions in the theater. They helped set up the base in the bare desert—digging bunkers, filling and stacking sandbags, driving trucks, and setting up communications equipment. At that point Corp. Deborah Yelle, a tactical satellite communications repairman, was surprised to find herself 100 miles closer to the potential front lines than her fiancé.

When the ground offensive started, the Marine infantry units leapfrogged past the forward support group to attack the entrenched enemy. They relied on the support troops, male and female, to keep them supplied with ammunition, fuel, and essential stores. According to the Corps' Commandant, Gen. Alfred M. Gray, Jr., his women, like his men in the theater, all performed their duties like "superb Marines."

The Air Force policies on assigning women were somewhat less complicated than those of the Army and Marine Corps but were often as contradictory. The law forbade women from flying on aircraft engaged in combat missions, which the Air Force interpreted as excluding women from bombers and fighters. But women were at the controls and in the crews of the jet tankers that refueled them in midair during attack missions. On one of her missions, Capt. Ann Weaver Worster flew her KC-135 tanker 250 miles into Iraq. The tankers constituted very easy and lucrative targets, since they were unarmed and loaded with precious fuel essential to the success of the air campaign. These lumbering giants were highly vulnerable to surface-to-air missiles and would have been sitting ducks for Iraqi fighters had the coalition forces not been able to gain air superiority early on. The same could have been said of the Airborne Warning and Control Systems (AWACS) aircraft directing the air traffic over the battlefield, and the transports delivering troops, supplies, and equipment. All were lucrative targets; all were defenseless; all were open to women.

In one of the more inexplicable anomalies of the war, Air Force women were routinely assigned to tactical air bases in Saudi Arabia, where they serviced, repaired, and armed combat aircraft in preparation for strike missions. The air bases were frequent targets of Iraqi Scud missile attacks and took direct hits. Navy women, on the other hand, were banned from assignments in any capacity on the aircraft carriers offshore. The missions of the bases and carriers were the same but the carriers had the protection of the entire fleet. The only exceptions for women on the carriers were those flying support aircraft bringing in personnel and supplies, but even they were not permitted to remain aboard.

Moreover, although Navy women were barred from serving on the crews of combat ships, female sailors were assigned aboard the ships that provided essential supplies, repair, and ammunition to the American fleet during Gulf combat operations. They were also aboard the hospital ships offshore. All of these support ships would have been as vulnerable to Exocet and Silkworm missiles and floating mines as the combat ships, and they generally sailed without the protection of the fleet.

After being exposed to the media coverage of the war and seeing women's performance on live TV, the American public and members of Congress understandably began to question the logic of the rules and laws governing women's participation in the military, particularly as they related to combat situations.

Some of the Faces of War

The real story of American women in the Gulf War is as much about individuals as about policies. Although their experiences were different by light-years from their predecessors in World Wars I and II, the women of Desert Storm were, nevertheless, pioneers exploring the new limits of a profession often hostile to their presence. Following are a few of their stories as soldiers, sailors, airmen, and Marines doing their jobs.

Capt. Stephanie Wells' credentials as a command pilot were impeccable. Few military pilots could match her combined experience in the active and reserve Air Force and in NASA. However, as tensions escalated in the Gulf, Wells feared she might have to sit this one out. On 6 August 1990, the day President Bush made the announcement that the United States would be sending troops to Saudi Arabia, Wells had called her reserve unit at Kelly Air Force Base in Texas and was told that women were being excluded. She was outraged. "Perhaps the Saudis have said no women," she reasoned. The next day the call came "women are NOT excluded." Within days she was flying C-5 missions all over the globe in support of the Gulf operation while still holding down her full-time job as staff instructor pilot with NASA at the Johnson Space Center in Houston, Texas.

On 29 August 1990, Wells' reserve unit, the 68th Military Airlift Squadron of the Military Airlift Command, was activated and she was given twenty-four hours to get her affairs in order and report for full active duty. Once activated, the 68th became part of the largest airlift operation in history. As a command pilot, Wells flew 600 hours in support of the operation. This included twenty-two flights into Saudi Arabia, Egypt, and the United Arab Emirates, on trips averaging fourteen days. Cargo consisted of helicopters, trucks, tanks, missiles (including Patriots), medical supplies, and food, as well as some troops. She also took trips to Thailand and into Turkey in support of the Kurd relief effort.

Sgt. Theresa Lynn Treloar, the "Ice Lady," earned her nickname by virtue of her direct, confident style and single-minded commitment to a tough and dangerous assignment—an assignment that put her closer to the battlefront than any other American woman on the ground in Iraq. So secret was her mission that her Army superiors refused to describe it or to permit photographs of her for publication. "I was given the opportunity to turn this job down," she told reporters. "I chose this and I knew what I was getting myself into when I chose it." According to Capt. Michael Mendell, the leader of the team of twenty-three men and one woman, "there were no other female soldiers in the same situation." Mendell had chosen Treloar for the assignment over the objections of higher headquarters. It was insisted that an assignment so close to the front lines would be against Army policy. The camp was only a few miles from the front, within range of Iraqi artillery. When American forces crossed the border, the unit would move forward and she with it. "She is the only woman I know who carries an M-16 rifle, a light antitank weapon, an AT-4 and grenade," Mendell said. "I would trust her to cover my back in any situation."

An outspoken, French-speaking soldier with a seven-year-old daughter at home and a "great marriage," Treloar believed that because she was a woman, some male soldiers were quick to misinterpret her professional manner for coldness and had dubbed her the "Ice Lady." The opposite male perception, she said, is that "anger in a woman reflects emotionalism."

The Persian Gulf was not the first time Treloar had challenged Army policy and attitudes. During Operation Just Cause, when her unit deployed to Panama, she had been forced to remain behind at Fort Bragg because of a battalion rule that forbade spouses from serving together on a mission. When her husband, Sgt. Charles Barbour, was sent to Panama, she said she confronted the officer who had written the rule and told him calmly that if the rule were imposed again she would divorce her husband. She meant it. "I would have just lived with my husband instead of being married to him."

Sergeant Treloar said she was proud to put her life on the line for "the American way of life" and was well aware that she was trailblazing for military women. "I always feel the pressure," she said. Her activities during Desert Storm remained classified even after the cease-fire.

Capt. Cynthia Mosley, thirty, commanded Alpha Company of the 24th Support Battalion Forward, 24th Infantry Division (Mechanized). The mission of the 100 men and women of her company was to supply a mechanized brigade with fuel, water, ammunition, and anything else it needed to operate in the field. During the ground assault, the company followed close behind the advancing forces on Highway 8 into Iraq. At one point, the combat units were advancing so rapidly that they were running out of fuel. As the support unit closest to the front, Alpha Company pulled up beside M1 tanks and Bradley fighting vehicles on the side of the road to refuel them so they could continue the attack. For a while, they were supporting not only the brigade they were assigned to, but all the brigades in that area of the front. The Army awarded Captain Mosley the Bronze Star medal for meritorious combat service.

Capt. Sheila G. Chewing was a weapons controller on one of the Air Force's AWACS aircraft that directed the air war over Iraq. On 17 January 1991 she helped shoot down two Iraqi fighters during one of the first dogfights of the war. During the first bombing raid on Baghdad, Chewing identified two Russian-built Iraqi MiG-29 interceptors and directed U.S. F-15 fighters in for the attack. Then she listened to the radio exchanges between the F-15 crews as they blew away the MiGs and called, "Splash two." It was the first of many such experiences for Chewing and the rest of the AWACS crews. "When that happened (bringing down an enemy plane), we really felt like we were doing our jobs."

Lt. Phoebe Jeter, twenty-seven had her moment of truth shortly after midnight on Tuesday, 21 January 1991, when she heard the words "Scud Alert" and the sirens went off. She had trained for three years in simulated war games for this moment. As commander of an all-male Patriot Delta Battery of "Scudbusters," Jeter knew that the alert was no drill—this was for real. The Scuds were coming into their area and could be carrying either chemical or conventional warheads. "Everybody was scared . . . we didn't know where they were headed." Within minutes her computer screen revealed that the Scuds were headed for her base and Riyadh. Jeter was in charge of the engagement control center from which Delta Battery's Patriots would be fired. She barked commands through her gas mask to her tactical control assistant, ordering thirteen missiles fired, which destroyed at least two Scuds.

The ultimate irony, of course, was that by the Army's Humpty Dumpty definition, Jeter and her men had not been in "combat."

Proud to be the first female Scudbuster, Lieutenant Jeter was one of the thousands of black women who served their country in the Gulf War. She was commissioned through the ROTC program and admits that she joined the Army looking for "adventure," but she learned in Saudi Arabia that, "I could do anything that I wanted to do."

Airman 1st Class Gina Maskunas-Delaney, of Killen, Texas, was a crew chief for an F-117 Stealth fighter. She scrawled a message to Saddam Hussein on the side of a laser-guided bomb being secured to the bay of her plane: "We care enough to send the very best."

Lt. Col. Ora Jane "O.J." Williams, forty-nine, from Monticello, Mississippi, was a career soldier with eighteen years in the Army when she deployed to the Gulf from Fort Bragg, North Carolina. Williams commanded the 2nd Material Management Center, a battalion-sized logistics management unit with the mission of requisitioning supplies for three combat divisions: the 24th Infantry Division (Mechanized), the 82nd Airborne, and the 101st Airborne. Her unit handled tens of thousands of daily requests for everything from ammunition and spare parts to food, tents, and clothing. "I'm here because I can do (the job)," she said confidently. Being the only female in the unit, the men sometimes would give Williams a hard time. But being black, female, and tall, Williams was used to being given a hard time. "The men are always thinking, 'Is she going to be a powder puff or is she going to pull her weight?' It doesn't make any difference," she said philosophically. "You have to earn respect and demonstrate your capabilities."

S. Sgt. Hattie Brown, thirty, of South Boston, Virginia, deployed to the Gulf as a radio operator with an air defense unit. Located at a site near the Kuwait border, she and the eight men under her supervision relayed battle reports from the field to the headquarters. "I've confronted the idea of death and I try not to be scared," said Brown, an expert marksman. "If I die, I hope I do it with pride, trying to get the enemy." Her greatest fear was making a mistake that would cost someone else's life. She planned to become a police officer after leaving the Army.

S. Sgt. Laura Long, twenty-seven, of Sandusky, Ohio, was a vehicle dispatcher with the 1st Tactical Fighter Wing in Desert Storm. She worried about her drivers during the Scud alerts, wondering if they were okay. As a supervisor, she felt that she had to stay calm so she could "be there for everybody." So, rather than run for shelter as she was supposed to, Long stayed at her post and called her drivers. She believed that if women were allowed to be in the front lines, they would do as well as anybody; if allowed to be fighter pilots, "we would be the best fighter pilots around." If she had had her way when she joined the Air Force, Long would have been flying one of the combat fighters. But she decided to settle for less. "Sometimes you have to take what you can get."

Lt. Col. Roslyn Goff, forty-one, commanded 800 soldiers of a combat support battalion. When it came time to move out through the minefields into Kuwait and Iraq, her men were as apprehensive of her ability to lead them into the battlefield as they were about the enemy. But, according to the Army citation for the Bronze Star medal after the war, Goff had "inspired her battalion to excellence under fire."

Sgt. Sherry Callahan was an assistant maintenance crew chief and boss of the team that maintained and prepared the F-15 fighter flown by the commander of the 1st Tactical Fighter Wing. She called the plane "Daphne." She was proud of the fact that it had not broken down since they got to the Gulf. "We wash it. We maintain it," she said. "We take care of it like a personal car. Except we can't take it home." Her biggest frustration as a mechanic was that, at 140 pounds, she sometimes did not have that extra bit of strength needed to fix some things right. She was grateful to the men she worked with, who she admitted helped her out a lot. "When you first get to a base in this (mechanic) specialty, the guys always have a question in their minds: Is she going to be able to carry her load?" she said. "But once they find out . . . they help you as much as they can."

Sgt. Carla Barbour-Clark, thirty, of Madison, Virginia, was a forklift operator assigned to the 438th Aerial Port Squadron out of McGuire Air Force Base in New Jersey. A divorced mother of a three-year-old daughter, Barbour-Clark worked twelve hours a day moving pallets at a sprawling air base in Saudi Arabia. When the Scuds came in, she said she thought her heart would stop. "That rush of adrenaline comes, and there's a moment of panic," she said. "I don my chem gear, and if I see someone who is having trouble with theirs, I help them."

S. Sgt. Cynthia Williams, of Glouster, Virginia, took exception to those who thought that women would not be able to hold their own in a combat situation. An air policeman with eleven years in the Air Force, Williams was assigned to the 1st Tactical Fighter Wing Security Police Squadron. Her job was to guard the gate to the air base in Saudi Arabia. Among the tools of her job was her M-16 rifle. She admitted that incoming Scuds gave her "a jolt" but that the threat of terrorism was more frightening. When asked if she would hesitate to use her weapon in a terrorist attack, Williams almost resented the question. "The gate guards are male and female alike," she said. "The women can be shot just like the men. I feel no hesitation in picking up an M-16 and going at it."

Prisoners of War

As had been predicted, women's integration into the operational elements of the armed forces would not come without a price. One of the nation's worst fears was realized on 31 January 1991 when the Iraqi government announced that it had captured an unspecified "number of male and female conscripts." Any female prisoner would receive "good treatment in accordance with the spirit of lofty Islamic laws." The only report of U.S. soldiers missing since the start of Desert Storm was of two members of a transportation battalion missing along an oil pipeline in the vicinity of the Saudi Arabia-Kuwait border. One was a woman.

Even before the POW report was officially confirmed, the experts began speculating on how an American woman might fare as a prisoner of the Iraqis. Although Army and Navy nurses imprisoned by the Japanese during World War II had not been mistreated, the U.S. military had been contending for years that any female taken prisoner by an enemy would be forced to endure unspeakable horrors. Observers of Arab culture, however, contended that a female POW might have less to fear than male prisoners because of the "revered" position of women in the Arab world. They might be exploited for propaganda purposes, but beating or sexual abuse was unlikely. "If they're (Iraqis) behaving based on the traditional laws of Arab society," observed Ashraf Ghani, an associate professor of anthropology at Johns Hopkins University in Baltimore, "they would go out of their way to be respectful to women." But he added that, considering Iraq had its back to the wall, "they might do anything."

"The ones least surprised by this are the women," said retired Brig. Gen. Evelyn Foote. "It's all part of the bargain of being a soldier, sailor, airman or marine," she said. "It was certainly on my mind when I was in Vietnam in 1967."

Spec. 4 Melissa Rathbun-Nealy, twenty, of Grand Rapids, Michigan, was identified by Pentagon officials three days after the Iraqi announcement that they had female prisoners. The Army said that she was one of two Army truck drivers missing in action and probably taken prisoner by the Iraqis. She thus acquired the dubious distinction of being the first American enlisted woman to become a prisoner of war, and the first U.S. female military POW since World War II.

Rathbun-Nealy had enlisted in 1989, according to her father, Leo Rathbun, because she did not have career goals at the time. She was stationed at Fort Bliss, Texas. When her unit, the 233rd Transportation Company, was deployed to Saudi Arabia in October 1991, she admitted to being scared but felt that women had the right to be in combat. After she got there she made it clear that she wanted to be close to the action if the war started. According to her father, "She told her supervisor that she didn't want to be stuck behind a desk. She wanted to do what she was trained to do." What she was trained to do was drive twenty-four-wheel trucks that transport tanks.

On 30 January 1991, Rathbun-Nealy and Spec. David Lockett were driving a heavy-duty Army truck carrying supplies when they became stuck in the sand and were overrun by Iraqi troops. Both were wounded by enemy fire—she by a bullet and shrapnel in her arm, he by bullets in his chest. They were first taken to Basra and then to Baghdad. They later described their most fearful time—during the coalition air raids when they could see the bombs exploding close by.

During her first telephone conversation with her anxious parents, Rathbun-Nealy assured them that the Iraqis had taken "excellent" care of her and described her captors as "beautiful people." Her guards had called her a hero as brave as Sylvester Stallone and as beautiful as Brooke Shields. Joan Rathbun asked her daughter if she realized just how famous she had become. "Well I'm beginning to get the idea," she replied.

Americans got their first glimpse of Rathbun-Nealy when she came down the steps of the plane in the first prisoner release. The baggy yellow prisoner's suit could not disguise her quiet composure and military bearing. Even General Schwarzkopf, the usually unruffled commander of the Coalition Forces, seemed tongue-tied as he greeted her at the foot of the airplane stairs.

Maj. Rhonda Cornum's capture went unnoticed until it was over. Prior to the POW exchange, there had been no mention in the press of a second American woman being taken prisoner. And even then only the first name gave the clue—Rhonda was clearly not a man's name.

The early reports of a Black Hawk helicopter being shot down indicated that all aboard were lost. No mention was made of any crew members being taken prisoner or that there had been women aboard. Gradually, information came out that there had been survivors, but there was still no mention that a woman was involved. Actually, three of the eight soldiers aboard survived and were taken prisoner, Cornum among them.

Cornum, thirty-six, an Army flight surgeon and mother of a fourteen-year-old daughter, was assigned to the 2nd Battalion, 229th Aviation Regiment at Fort Rucker, Alabama, when both she and her husband, Air Force Capt. Kory Cornum, were deployed to the Persian Gulf.

On 27 February 1991 the call came from operations to the pilot of the ill-fated Black Hawk helicopter for a mission to rescue a downed F-16 pilot sixty miles away in Iraq. The pilot had been injured in the crash. "You have Doc Cornum on board? Do you have all of your equipment?" "Yeah," the chopper pilot replied. Cornum later recounted what happened next:

> We flew as fast as we could, over a bunch of our guys, moving east. A few minutes after we saw the last friendly convoy, we started taking small-arms and anti aircraft fire. Seconds later we got hit, then we crashed.
>
> After we tumbled and rolled, I found myself underneath at least part of the wreck. I wasn't thinking clearly enough to know why I couldn't use my arms. I used one foot to kind of push my way out from underneath this airplane: By the time I got out, the Iraqi soldiers were there.

After the crash, Cornum heard a flurry of Arabic when they pulled off her helmet. That was when the Iraqis realized that their captive was a woman. "They were surprised, although not as surprised . . . as Saudi soldiers would have been," she said. "There are female nurses in the Iraqi military." Cornum was thrown over the tailgate into the back of a truck, unable to cushion the fall with her arms.

She and one of her fellow survivors, Sgt. Troy Dunlap, were first taken to Baath Party headquarters and then on to Baghdad, where they joined the third survivor, who was also injured. Except for being thrown into the truck, Cornum said that she had not been mistreated. She was given medical care to stabilize her broken arms but she would not allow the Iraqis to perform the surgery she knew was required. Her biggest problem, other than the pain, was her one-piece flight suit. With the condition of her arms she could not remove the suit to take care of normal personal necessities, and the Iraqi guards did not want to help her undress. It would have been wrong for an Iraqi man to see any part of her body. Finally, a guard took pity on her: He put a large bag over her head and helped unzip her flight suit as the bag came down. Later, Dunlap was able to assist her. "Dunlap was a real star," she later reported.

Cornum was released with other prisoners on 6 March. She was a happy but odd vision as she stepped carefully off the plane in her yellow POW garb, both arms in slings, her long hair hanging in an unmilitary fashion down her back. But Cornum never lost her characteristic cool as the crowd, led by General Schwarzkopf, greeted her and the other released POW's. How was she feeling, someone called out. "Airborne!" she shouted.

Doctor, surgeon, paratrooper, pilot, Army officer, mother, hero. "God, she's tough, she's tough," her mother said. "She could always do anything and she still will."

The two former women POWs, Rathbun-Nealy and Cornum, met briefly aboard the hospital ship *Mercy*. What was it like to meet one another? a reporter asked later. "We're both females in the Army. That's about it," Cornum replied matter-of-factly. "Gender doesn't come into play at all, to tell the truth. Nor did it the whole war, which I think is the most important thing you can come away with."

Death Did Not Discriminate

In the end, Melissa Rathbun-Nealy and Rhonda Cornum could count themselves among the lucky ones. Thirteen other women would not make it home alive.

The first American women to die in a war since Vietnam and the first enlisted women ever to be killed in action perished with twenty-five of their male comrades on the night of 25 February 1991, when a Scud missile slammed into the military barracks near Dhahran.

Spec. Beverly Clark, twenty-three, of Armagh, Pennsylvania, was part of an extremely close family of three sisters and a brother. She had joined the Army right after graduating from high school. When news of her death came, her hometown was in shock. "She just was a fine all-around human being," said a former employer. "There's been a lot of tears (here)."

Spec. Christine Mayes, twenty-two, of Rochester Mills, Pennsylvania, had gotten engaged just the day before leaving for the Gulf. "She didn't really want to be over there any more than the rest of them." said her fiancé, David Fairbanks. "But that's what she got paid for; that's what she did."

Spec. Adrienne L. Mitchell, twenty, of Moreno Valley, California, had just wanted to get out on her own, "to finance her own education," explained her mother. Her father, retired Air Force Chief Master Sgt. Frank Mitchell, had not wanted Adrienne to join the Army. But, like so many young people attracted to the military, she wanted to earn money for a college education under the GI Bill. After initial training she was assigned to the 475th Quartermaster Battalion at Fort Lee, Virginia, and deployed with it to Saudi Arabia. Although Frank Mitchell said he was all for women in the military, he did not approve of their serving in a combat theater. "I just do not think that the U.S. male population is ready for women in combat." Adrienne wrote home to her worried parents that she wasn't scared. "The only thing we've got to worry about is the Scud missiles." Three days later the word came that their daughter was gone. "I did 30 years . . . and didn't get a scratch," her father said. "My daughter's been in for five months, and she's dead."

Maj. Marie T. Rossi, thirty-two, and the three men in her crew were killed on 1 March 1991, the day after the cease-fire, when her Chinook chopper hit an unlit tower at night in bad weather. When the news of her death was flashed by the media, millions of Americans felt that they had lost one of their own. On 24 February, the eve of the massive ground assault into Iraq, Rossi had stolen the hearts of TV viewers during an interview on CNN. "Sometimes you have to disassociate how you feel personally about the prospect of going into war and . . . possibly see the death that is going to be out there," she had said. "But . . . this is the moment that everybody trains for—that I've trained for—so I feel ready to meet the challenge."

Siblings and friends recall that even as a child, Marie was a natural leader and instigator, who was looking for new things. So no one was surprised when she entered Army ROTC and, in 1980, graduated as a second lieutenant. After serving briefly as an artillery officer, she went on to become a helicopter pilot. While flying Chinooks in South Korea she met John "Andy" Cayton, a Warrant Officer helicopter pilot. They subsequently married and had the rare good fortune to be together in Saudi Arabia, but flying in different units.

Rossi was one of the first American Army helicopter pilots to fly into enemy territory delivering troops, supplies, ammunition, and fuel to the front. She had made several flights into Iraq facing hostile fire and had come away without a scratch. "After the TV interview, we were so excited and proud," said her father, Paul Rossi. "Then came the awful news—Marie's not coming home." Her mother, Gertrude, said that is was hard to accept, but "I know Marie. My daughter would expect us not to fall apart."

Warrant Officer Ken Copley, helicopter pilot and veteran of the Vietnam War, who had known Marie in her previous assignment, paid her the ultimate pilot's compliment: She was one of the most respected pilots he had ever known.

Sgt. Cheryl LaBeau-O'Brien, twenty-four, of Racine, Wisconsin, made the ultimate sacrifice when the Black Hawk helicopter she served on as a crew member was shot down near the Iraqi border.

Cheryl and her husband, Michael, probably considered themselves fortunate in that they had both deployed to the Persian Gulf and were stationed in the desert only two miles apart. Cheryl loved her job servicing helicopters in the 1st Infantry Division. When she died it was doing what she wanted to do. Her mother, Lois LaBeau, had been concerned about her daughter's safety but had been told that Cheryl would be many miles behind the front lines. But knowing how committed her daughter was, Lois was not reassured. "I knew that if something needed to be done, she would never say, 'No, I'm not going. That's a combat zone.'" Michael agreed: "Cheryl wouldn't have said, 'Let it be a man.' Cheryl would have said, 'Let it be me.'"

Capt. Terry VandenDolder, an Air Force reserve pilot called up to fly C-141 transports for the airlift, flew home twenty-two bodies of fallen American soldiers. Two were women. "There was great sadness and grief for the lives cut short by war but no more for the women than for the men," she says. "There were tears for each."

WOMEN UNDER FIRE[2]

They drive trucks and fly helicopters; direct missile launches and command ground crews. Since the Persian Gulf crisis began last August, America's military women have been playing an extraordinary part in Operation Desert Shield. Every night on TV

[2]Article by Andrea Gross, from *Ladies Home Journal*, D 1990, 107:93+. © Copyright 1990, Andrea Gross & Meredith Corporation. Reprinted with permission.

newscasts, we see them slogging through the Saudi Arabian sands in desert camouflage, lugging the same bulky sixty-six-pound rucksacks as their male comrades. We witness all the touching family farewells of young mothers who've been called—so many, in fact, that this has been nicknamed "the Moms' war."

Clearly, it's not "this man's Army"—or Navy or Marines or Air Force—anymore. As the Mideast conflict has vividly illustrated, women have made themselves essential to the U.S. Armed Forces. They're performing a wider range of duties than ever before, and in places where they used to be barred. Just seven years ago, four Army military policewomen who had arrived in Grenada after the invasion were quickly sent home again until the worst was over; today, it's estimated that up to 11 percent of U.S. forces in the Gulf—or as many as fifteen thousand troops—are female. "This crisis will demonstrate to people that women are an integral part of the armed forces, that we couldn't do the job without them," says Lawrence Korb, former assistant secretary of defense for manpower under the Reagan administration.

Not only are they doing their part, but they're carrying an extra burden: the hostility of many Saudis to American-style equality. Saudi women do not drive, wear shorts or work among men; to avoid offending an ally, U.S. servicewomen are sweltering in long sleeves instead of T-shirts, skipping their jogging routines and running errands only in the company of a man. "Women are living a much harder life than the men because of these restrictions," says Congresswoman Pat Schroeder (D-Colo.), a senior member of the House Armed Services committee and a leading advocate for military women. "If they can do their jobs under these conditions, they can do their jobs anywhere."

Womanpower has been a long time coming to the military; twenty-five years ago, females made up only 1.2 percent of the personnel and served mostly in traditional fields like nursing and administration. Then, in 1973, the U.S. abandoned the draft. Short of male volunteers, the Pentagon turned to women to fill in the gap.

Today, the 230,000 women on active duty make up 11 percent of all American service personnel, and their job descriptions have expanded to include teaching jet-fighter pilots how to fly and raw recruits how to shoot. "I let them know I can do anything," says Army Sergeant Lisa Rudolph, twenty-seven, of Fort Jackson, South Carolina, who was this year's runner-up in the national drill-sergeant competition. "I am capable of training them, teaching them what they need to know and beating them at a race—and they learn to respect me."

Remarkable as these advances are, servicewomen still have a long way to go. Because they're forbidden to be part of a combat unit—by law in the Navy, Air Force and Marines, and by policy in the Army—women confront a bewildering array of conflicting policies. They can serve on Navy supply ships, for example, but not on combat ships patrolling the same enemy waters; they can refuel planes or fly troops over enemy territory, but not command fighter planes in the same skies. Many women feel these limitations relegate them to the status of second-class soldiers and hamper career advancement.

Soldiers—and mothers

Whatever the obstacles to progress, women are enlisting in record numbers. Why? Mostly, they want to serve for the same reasons men do. Patriotism is one, of course, mixed with the desire for a little adventure. "I'm trained for it, and now that the real stuff is happening, I want to go so bad," confides Army Staff Sergeant Teresa Irizarry, now an administrator at Fort Sheridan, Illinois.

Many also join because—however restricted it might be—a military career seems to offer them the best chance for education and self-fulfillment. "When I was eighteen, I had a choice," says Lieutenant Colonel Loretta Behrens, of Lackland Air Force Base, in Texas. "I could either join the military and see the world, or stay in Clarksville [Texas] and be a waitress." In her twenty years of service, she has completed college, spent several years in both Europe and Asia, and is a squadron commander in charge of nearly three hundred people, about three-quarters of whom are men.

Military life is not always so fulfilling in family terms, however. Yes, there are subsidized day-care centers and good schools at many bases, as well as subsidized housing and inexpensive shopping at the PX. But the demands of the job are unparalleled. Military personnel often put in twelve-or fourteen-hour workdays. They can be ordered to report to work at three in the morning, respond to a midnight alert or go into the field for days at a time. In the case of an emergency, like the Persian Gulf crisis, they may have to deploy on fewer than fifteen hours' notice. Often, family must take second place.

"It's hard," says Army Sergeant Patricia Tudor, twenty-two, who has a two-year-old daughter, Aimée. "It's *very* hard." Tudor and her husband, Jaime, are both medical specialists (similar to paramedics), and both were shipped out from Fort Ord, California, to Panama last year for thirty-two days.

Luckily, Tudor was able to convince her regular day-care helper to move in and watch over Aimée while her parents were gone. (Like all servicewomen who have husbands in the military or are single mothers, Tudor was required to appoint a legal guardian to care for her child in case she is deployed or killed.) She knows she might be sent away again at any moment. And while she understands her duty, the prospect worries her nonetheless. "We all knew what we were getting into [when we joined the Army], and it's part of the job and all that, but . . . " Her voice breaks. "*Me* going? Please, I have a little girl . . . "

Fighting for their rights

Military women also confront career challenges that are familiar to civilian women as well—sexual harassment and job discrimination. The Pentagon recently released the results of its first major study of sexual harassment in the military: Of 9,500 women surveyed, two out of three women reported harassment from colleagues. Another study revealed that three out of four women in the Air Force—regarded as the most equality-minded of all the armed forces branches—had experienced sexual discrimination or harassment (anything from a sexist comment to inappropriate touching or overtures). While some predict that this problem will fade with the retirement of older officers—presumed to be more rigid in their thinking—there are signs that all is not well among younger leaders, either. Last December, just before the annual Army-Navy football game at Annapolis, two male midshipmen forcibly handcuffed classmate Gwen Marie Dreyer, nineteen, to a urinal and snapped pictures of her while a group of other young men looked on and jeered. The instigators were later punished with one month's loss of leave time and demerits on their records; six of the onlookers received written reprimands.

A disillusioned Dreyer resigned from the Academy, citing both the bathroom incident and the treatment of women in general. Superintendent Rear Admiral Virgil Hill, Jr., then announced the would "try very hard to prevent violations of human rights," while adding, "but we also accept the fact that mistakes will happen."

Military women who are suspected of being lesbians are particularly vulnerable to harassment. Homosexuality remains grounds for automatic discharge from the armed services, but according to the Pentagon's own statistics, women are about three times more likely to be dismissed because of homosexuality than are men. "Lesbian-baiting is one way to get women out of the military," says Paula Ettelbrick, legal director for Lambda Legal Defense and Education Fund, a national lesbian- and gay-rights organization.

Army Major Hope Gentle, forty-three and single, says that she has been victimized by this attitude. Two years ago, talk-show personality Geraldo Rivera hosted a segment on "Gays in Uniform." One of his guests was a woman who rents part of Gentle's Wisconsin home; another guest remained anonymous, hidden behind a screen. Army investigators believed Gentle was the unseen woman.

"They don't go after confirmed felons with the same fervor with which I've been tracked," Gentle says. According to Gentle, who says she has seen her file, investigators checked with the Federal Aviation Administration and two airlines to see if she had flown to New York prior to the show's taping; they interviewed the drivers of the limousine service that transports Rivera's guests, and they checked the guest register of a Manhattan hotel. "They can't prove it was me, but I can't prove it *wasn't*," says Gentle, who insists she is not a lesbian. During the investigation, which lasted more than two years, her security clearance was suspended, and despite seventeen years of exemplary service, she has yet to be promoted to lieutenant colonel.

The last tree house

For any woman, promotion to the higher ranks remains difficult; many say they run smack into a "brass ceiling." For example, of the top one thousand sixty-four officers in the military, only eight are women. Some Pentagon officials argue that these discouraging statistics will improve by the end of the decade, when the bulk of female officers will have been in the service twenty-five years—the time it typically takes to achieve high rank.

Still, the highest barrier for women remains combat exclusion. "The policy says that women are different and, in fact, less valuable," says Patricia Ireland, executive vice-president of the National Organization for Women (NOW). "The military's job is ultimately to be prepared for combat, and the automatic presumption is that women can't cut it."

Because of the exclusion, women cannot assume the high-profile leadership positions that usually assure promotion. Complains Marine Corps Captain Mariana Pearson, an aircraft maintenance officer, "One of my peers, a man, was with a squadron that went to the Persian Gulf during the Iran-Iraq war. He got a combat fitness report and a medal for that. I will never have the opportunity to have that kind of thing in my record, even though he was doing the exact same job there, on a ship, that I'm doing here at Camp Pendleton. All other things being equal, he will have the edge when it comes to promotions." There is pride at stake, too, says Pearson. "Why is it acceptable for my buddy, who's a guy, to be in danger and not me? I can do the same job, and we are all in this together."

Some supporters of the policy argue that women are not physically strong enough to handle combat gear such as sixty-pound shells that are loaded into large guns; others contend that the presence of females would somehow interrupt male bonding and willingness to fight. Still others say the country isn't ready to see women killing or being killed (though in fact, this is not far from reality now; many service-women are carrying arms in the Mideast, and there have been female casualties in every war fought by the U.S. in this century).

Last January, after several Army women were lauded for their courageous actions during the Panama invasion, Congresswoman Schroeder proposed a four-year test during which the Army would integrate women into its combat units. The bill never made it out of subcommittee. "This is the last tree house," says Schroeder. "It's the one place where a man can still post a 'No Girls Allowed' sign and women are forced to obey it."

Schroeder believes, though, that the Mideast crisis, along with technology, is blurring all the distinctions between front- and rear-line jobs, and she plans to reintroduce her bill in the next session of Congress. Women are already at risk in the Persian Gulf, she notes, since they serve in the vital communications, supply and refueling centers that are often the first targets of an attack. "If it gets to a combat situation, the women are going to be there," she says. "We're not going to be able to bring them all back if the shooting starts."

Indeed, many women see the conflict as a chance to prove themselves once and for all. Says Carrie Sullivan, a sergeant at Camp Pendleton who has volunteered for Middle East duty, "I don't want to be a pretend Marine. I want to sweat right along with the men. I want to feel I've contributed."

Whatever the outcome of the standoff in Saudi Arabia, America's servicewomen have already won a major victory by making their contributions impossible to ignore.

THE RIGHT TO FIGHT[3]

To many feminists, the armed forces have been a model for change. A woman has been selected head cadet at West Point. During the Persian Gulf War, women commanders led troops through minefields in the desert. On base, day-care centers are standard issue. But despite these advances, women are still locked out of the heart of the military: combat. Many military women complain that combat is the missing step on their career ladders. "Instead of a glass ceiling, they have a lead ceiling," says Carolyn Becraft, a military consultant for the Women's Research and Education Institute, a Washington, D.C., think tank. But many other female soldiers and sailors say they don't want the right to kill. According to a NEWSWEEK Poll, Americans are almost equally split on the issue. While 52 percent of those surveyed said women should be assigned to ground-combat units, 44 percent said no. And only 26 percent thought women should be assigned to combat on the same terms as men.

[3]Article by Barbara Kantrowitz with Eleanor Clift and John Barry, from *Newsweek*, Ag 5, 1991, 118:22-23. © 1991, Newsweek, Inc. Reprinted with permission.

This week Congress will take up the debate when the Senate considers an amendment to this year's defense authorization bill allowing women to fly fighter planes. The proposal easily passed the House in May. Supporters say they've heard very few "Hell, no's"—a measure of progress for such a controversial topic. Still, Lawrence Korb, a defense analyst, thinks the Senate will recommend that a commission study the issue, a course that all sides agree is a delaying tactic. "There's never been a group studied more than women in the military, and they do very well," says Rep. Patricia Schroeder (Democrat of Colorado) who cosponsored the House plan. "But everyone still says they don't want them there. How do you deal with that?"

There are hawks and doves on both sides of this issue, but conservative Republicans are the most outspoken opponents of women in combat. "The thought of a woman parachuting out over downtown Baghdad or Hanoi strikes horror into my heart," says California Rep. Robert Dornan. He predicts that coming cuts in the size of the U.S. military will doom any expansion of women's roles. "The chance of reaching out for any kind of affirmative action is nil to zero," he says. "And that goes for homosexuals and lesbians too." But even without the cutbacks, Dornan says, "If I had 200 fighter pilots and an Amelia Earhart came along . . . I would still pick the man."

Within the military itself, recent Senate hearings showed an attitude gap between officers and enlisted men. Higher-ranked men said they thought women could comfortably fill in as pilots, submarine captains or on helicopter crews—tasks that require brains, skill and a killer temperament. Men on the grunt level were the most resistant. They said the vast majority of women aren't strong enough for fighting on the front lines. There's also a generation gap. "The people making these decisions are elderly males who don't understand young people," says Korb. "They didn't play soccer with women and go to school with them. They don't understand there's not a sexual overtone in every encounter."

Wild tales: The current proposal wouldn't put women in ground combat. Even some of those who support lifting the ban on fighter-pilot jobs say they would be reluctant to take that final move right now. Conservative Democrat Beverly Byron, who cosponsored the House proposal with Schroeder, would stop at combat flying while Schroeder thinks all barriers should go. In the Senate, Strom Thurmond of South Carolina agrees that women can be fighter pilots, but he, too, draws the line at ground combat. There's also some doubt among military women themselves about ground fighting. "There aren't too many women who want to go into the infantry," says Korb. Many men in the infantry say women would ruin male bonding among the troops, the emotional tie they say is crucial to effective fighting. To Becraft, that sounds similar to the argument used against full integration of blacks after World War II: that whites wouldn't feel "comfortable." "There goes the neighborhood," she quips.

Since the passage of the House bill there's been a fierce whispering campaign on Capitol Hill, with wild tales of women's misdeeds in the gulf—everything from rumors of women soldiers turning tricks to stories about the high number of pregnancies (36) aboard a single Navy ship. When asked about the floating maternity wing, Schroeder retorted: "Unless there was a star shining over that ship, I'd say it takes two . . . What kind of military discipline do we have that we blame only the women?"

When the smoke clears, Congress will probably choose a middle road that reflects the opinion of a majority of voters. In a NEWSWEEK Poll, 63 percent of respondents thought that it would be an advantage to have women pilot jet fighters; 61 percent said women would be an asset on bomber crews. And lifting the ban on flying fighter planes won't dramatically alter women's roles. They already fly support planes on combat missions, and already are in danger of being shot down. In the Persian Gulf, two women were taken prisoner and 11 were killed, five in action.

If the ban on flying in combat is lifted, women may look to Capt. Troy Devine for a role model. Captain Devine, a 1985 graduate of the Air Force Academy, is at the controls of one of the high-flying TR-1 spy planes that belong to the Ninth Strategic Reconnaissance Wing at Beale Air Force Base in California. In order to earn that privilege, she agreed not to become pregnant for at least a year and to submit to pregnancy tests every two weeks. It costs more than a half-million dollars to train a spy-plane pilot and the Air Force wants to protect its investment. There's also the risk of damage to a fetus from solar radiation at the plane's high altitude. But Captain Devine doesn't think of herself as a pioneer. Like thousands of other military women, she's just doing her job.

WAR AND THE SECOND SEX

The fight was inevitable. The gulf war and the 1989 Panama invasion put servicewomen in the middle of the shooting and the bleeding in a way no previous American war did. More than 35, 000 women served in the gulf—and discovered that modern warfare with its wide-ranging maneuver tactics and its long-range weaponry has blurred the old boundaries between "front" and "rear." Women worked in supply units, flew support aircraft, crewed Patriot and Hawk missile units and served aboard Navy tenders. These were not jobs with high combat probability. But 11 women were killed and two taken prisoner. Maj. Marie T. Rossi died when her chopper crashed while on a support mission. Army Specialist Melissa Rathbun-Nealy fell into enemy hands after accidentally driving into Iraqi positions in the desert. Three women died when an Iraqi Scud missile struck their billet near the end of the war. And so the argument: women already share the risks, let them fight equally alongside men. Let women be warriors, too.

The 1948 Combat Exclusion Act precludes women from combat roles in the U.S. Navy, Air Force and Marines. Army policy has the same restriction. Women are not allowed to fly combat aircraft in war zones and are banned from fighting ships. Combat infantry and armor units are closed to them. Now lawmakers led by Reps. Patricia Schroeder and Beverly Byron, joined by Sens. Edward Kennedy and William Roth, want to overturn the rule—with a Senate vote scheduled this week. And while many female officers support the move, other women say thanks, but no thanks—particularly in the enlisted ranks. "Tell Pat Schroeder to get out of my boots," snaps Maj. Kathleen Shields of the 70th Division, a 17-year Army reservist. "She's never been in the service and doesn't know what she's talking about." "I'm not getting in her boots and I don't intend to," says Schroeder. "I'm ensuring her equality and removing barriers to her opportunity."

Few topics I have dealt with as a veteran of Korea and Vietnam, and as a correspondent in the gulf war stir such emotions.

[3]Article by Col. David H. Hackworth, author of "About Face" and retiree from the U.S. Army in 1971. From *Newsweek*, Ag 5, 1991, 118:24-27. © 1991, Newsweek, Inc. Reprinted with permission.

Two sets of values are on a collision course. Equality and opportunity are noble ideals, but they have little to do with the battlefield, where the issues are living and dying. The question is: what if it turns out that equality and opportunity hurt combat readiness? The issue is not female bravery the gulf war proved that patriotism and heroism are not gender-dependent. It isn't professionalism. The women troops I met during and after the war are smart, dedicated and technically competent. They are also better educated than their male counterparts. I myself have no problem with women in combat flying attack aircraft, though many combat-experienced pilots offer strong arguments against it. I do know from eight years of ground combat that few women could endure its savagery for long. The issue was summed up in Senate testimony by Gen . Robert Barrow of the Marine Corps . It is not "about women's rights, equal opportunity, career assignments for enhancement purposes for selection to higher rank. It is about, most assuredly . . . combat effectiveness, combat readiness; and so we're talking about national security."

For this article I interviewed hundreds of service people of both sexes, some individually, many in groups. I went to five major U.S. bases. Women made up 20 percent of some units. I met a few I wouldn't want to arm-wrestle with, and a number I would have been proud to have at my side in a fire fight. Not many would actually choose to join the outfits that do the killing. "Only a small minority want combat units," says paratrooper M/Sgt. Penny Sweeny of Fort Bragg, N.C. "Women don't grow up playing with GI Joe dolls." But they hated the discrimination in the law: they wanted the right to combat. They compared it with the abortion issue: a woman's choice. Their anger reminded me of the controlled rage I saw in the 1960s among black soldiers who were kept down. Military women are also in the grip of a Catch-22. They need combat experience to get the top jobs, but the system won't give it to them. Navy Lt. Brenda Holdener, a helicopter pilot at Norfolk Air Station, was candid about this before a recent hearing of the Senate Armed Services Committee: "I am very selfish . . . I would like to see [the law] changed just because that would afford me more opportunities."

In fact, many combat opportunities could be opened to women. There are few tasks in the Navy that most women couldn't do. The SEALs require exceptional strength and stamina even by masculine standards, and submariners live in a claustrophobic world best suited to single-sex existence. In the Air Force, females are already well represented in 97 percent of the job assignments. USAF Col. Douglas Kennett at the Pentagon says that his service "couldn't go to war without women and we couldn't win without them." High-speed fighter aircraft do place demands on the physical strength of pilots: withstanding the force of 9Gs is no easy feat. But except for these jobs, the Navy and Air Force are high-tech services engaging mostly in standoff battles. Combatants never really see each other. Women can plot coordinates and push buttons as fast as men. But war will also continue to be about seizing ground, or defending it. In the gulf war, a badly led Iraqi Army allowed itself to be defeated by technology. Ground forces played a secondary role. This was a unique war, not a model. The next one may be less hospitable to high-tech weapons. Ground war is not dead. The line doggies will still engage the enemy eyeball to eyeball, belly to belly. And in that setting, women are disadvantaged. Brawn will count for more than computer smarts for a while yet. A 110-pound woman with the heart of a lion can't pack out a wounded 200-pound comrade. Army studies show that only 18 percent of women recruits could lift between 50 and 100 pounds. A grunt's rifle, ammunition and gear average 110. Tank and artillery rounds weigh between 50 and 100 pounds. "The issue is not strength," wrote Army Sgt. Donna Patzer of Tripler Army Medical Center, Hawaii, "but whether women are capable of performing the task which they are expected to perform."

The biggest complaint I heard from both women and men was there is one physical standard for men and another for women. Each service has a different standard for men and women, called gender norming. To get the Army's maximum fitness rating, for example, a 22-year-old male must be able to run two miles in 12 minutes and 36 seconds; a female gets an extra three minutes to win the same rating. To pass the Marines' combat-conditioning test, men must climb 20 feet of rope in 30 seconds; women can take 50 seconds. "We are told to evaluate woman on a different scale than man," says a male Air Force captain. "A woman who is adequate is rated as outstanding, or who is unacceptable is rated as acceptable . . . We lie to the public, we lie to the Air Force, and most of all we lie to each other." Schroeder agrees: "When the military imposes double standards, they think they're doing women a favor, but women don't want it."

'I can do it': The temptation is to say that women should be admitted to any combat role if they have the skills and the strength. Former New York mayor Edward Koch used to say he didn't care what sex his firefighters were so long as they could carry a 206-pound mayor out of a burning room. Lt. Margaret Dunn, an Air Defense Artillery leader in the gulf, got as close to combat as a woman could. She says that "not just any female can handle the physical and mental stress of a combat unit." But she feels herself fully capable. In 10 years of rising from the ranks, she has seen a change in male mind-set as women prove themselves, and a "woman must prove herself more than a man." Dunn is ramrod-lean and rucks 12 miles with a heavy pack. She maxes any fitness test on the male scale. "I don't see why I can't go [into combat]," she says. "I can do it."

But skill and strength are not the only issues. The top officers who opposed the Schroeder legislation were united on one point: the military has seen enough experimentation for the moment. The services are downsizing on a scale unseen since the end of World War II. They are restructuring units and redefining missions. They are intensively studying the lessons of the gulf war. It is strongly believed by the top brass that now isn't the time to put women into combat without first sorting out what is known and unknown about the issue, especially the intangibles such as effects on morale and unit cohesion. An Israeli colonel, asked by a visiting U.S. Army major, Martin Stanton, about the wisdom of using women in combat, said, "You can perhaps afford such experiments. *We* have to take war seriously."

The Army has changed since I wore a soldier's suit. It is now a big family where the married outnumber the single and the day-care center has replaced the day room. Dual-service parents are common. Back in 1971, women soldiers were WACs and fewer than 20,000 dedicated women mainly took care of sick people and paperwork. The end of the draft in 1973 opened the services up to women; there weren't enough male soldiers who were up to handling the complex jobs. Today the Army is the most sexually integrated of the services. Women do everything but kill enemy soldiers. Yet if attacked they know how to fight in a defensive role. I asked a woman captain if she felt like she had invaded the sacred turf of man. She replied, "It's not sacred anymore."

'Male bonding': Men's attitudes are changing, but slowly. During the gulf war many line commanders refused female medics—until they learned it was "take woman medics or go without." Thousands of years of genetic imprinting and social programming are at work. "I was raised to protect the female," says Specialist Peter Cardin of the elite XVIII Airborne Corps. "I couldn't handle being in a tank or infantry squad with a woman. It would blow unit esprit and destroy male bonding." Male bonding is an abstract thing, yet it is the glue that holds fighting units together and allows them to do the impossible. Once, after a night battle in Korea, every member of my Raider unit, including myself, lay dead or wounded. Not one survivor left his position—even though some were blind or had limbs shot off—so great was their dedication to their comrades. Spirit and will are the most essential elements of warfare. Without them you lose. At the end, we lacked them in Vietnam and we lost.

Ask the Israelis. They are the only ones with extensive experience of women in direct combat roles. The Israeli Army put women on the front lines in 1948. The experiment ended disastrously after only three weeks. It wasn't that the women couldn't fight. It was that they got blown apart. Female casualties demoralized the men and gutted unit cohesion. The men placed themselves at higher risks in order to protect women, and in some cases failed in their combat mission. Today, Israeli women are drafted, but not for direct combat jobs. Granted, things have changed since 1948. But no Pentagon order can abolish these fundamental attitudes. "The politicians are rushing the cadence," says Capt. Gloria Nickerson of the Special Warfare Center at Fort Bragg. "Nothing is going to change until society stops raising little girls to be popular and wear pink dresses and raising little boys to take care of little girls."

No holes: It's down at the bottom where the first sergeant and chief petty officer sit where the problems come home. The NCOs are the backbone of the military, they train, discipline and lead units into battle. It is here where ideas and policies are put into practice. Unlike the officers, NCOs don't shift units frequently. When the buck comes to a screeching halt, it's on their watch. It is here where readiness means moving prepared teams quickly with all their gear to do the job. Military teams—just like an urban police SWAT team—cannot have holes in them, every member is interdependent on the other. A rifle squad needs every member, as does a tank, aircraft, fighting ship and support and service unit. The military is serious business and with the drawdown and return to Fortress America, readiness is even more critical.

During Desert Shield all four services fielded units with crucial jobs unfilled. Some of these jobs had been assigned to single parents, others to a parent with a spouse also in the service. In all, there were more than 128,000 dual-service parents and single parents on active duty during the war. Many of these were slated for shipment to the gulf but had to stay home when a family-support plan fell apart. Parents would show up at the orderly room with children in tow. Many parents reached the gulf but then had to return home to sort out family problems. Others suffered psychologically for leaving their children. All this stress can't help but impair a combat soldier's effectiveness. In a NEWSWEEK Poll, 89 percent of the respondents were concerned by the idea of mothers with young children being sent to war.

Pregnancy is a perennial problem now. Between 10 and 15 percent of the servicewomen wear maternity uniforms during a normal year. It's hard to get precise numbers, as the Pentagon treats this information with almost as much sensitivity as it devotes to the location of nuclear weapons. But there is no question that pregnancy soared during the war. Three Pentagon sources report that as of mid-February of 1991, more than 1,200 pregnant women had been evacuated from the gulf—the equivalent of two infantry battalions. "Nineteen ninety-two will be a baby-boomer year," predicts one doctor at Andrews Air Force Base in Maryland. A Navy report says: "Pregnancy is viewed as epidemic." One ship alone, the destroyer tender Acadia, become known as the "Love Boat" after 36 female crew members conceived. An Army support company commander at Fort Bragg told me that out of 100 soldiers he had 13 pregnant women stay behind, which left a big hole in his unit. "Fortunately," he says, "the enemy gave us six months to fill those holes, or we would have been in a world of hurts."

Simple rule: Most senior commanders sent the pregnant women home. On the other hand, I have talked to women soldiers who got pregnant while in the gulf and who told no one and stuck it out because "they didn't want to let their team down." Other women soldiers had their babies and six weeks later rejoined their desert units. They, too, didn't want to let their units down. Too many woman soldiers say bitterly that their units "kept exacting statistics on pregnancy, but not on men's sport's injuries," which, according to Col. Robert Poole, the physician who headed the triage center at Andrews AFB, was the biggest casualty producer in the gulf. Schroeder says pregnancy in the service was "just not a problem," but the view at the bottom is that it was. Back in the days of the WACs, the senior women officers who ran that outfit had a simple rule: if you're pregnant you're out. Combat would intensify the problem. As Korean War machine-gunner Robert Haas puts it, "If a pregnant women catches a slug in the gut, what's the statistic: one dead soldier or two?"

The gulf experience revealed other problems:

• Fraternization. Put young men and women together for long stretches in the moonlike desert and they'll do do what's natural. The military issued more than a million condoms.

• Sexual harassment. Many women soldiers reported nightmare times. "There were hard stares and harder hits," explained a woman signaler. "Some guys hadn't seen a woman for five months and they acted like animals . . . They assumed we were [already] doing it."

There were even reports of rape and female prostitution that required courtsmartial. (However, owing to the absence of drugs and alcohol, the incidence of crime was much lower in the gulf than in the peacetime military or any other war.)

Few of the women who served in combat support units recommend the experience. Conditions get primitive when you near the cutting edge. Everyone complained about the sand, the grime and the heat, but women found the lack of privacy particularly hard. Bathing and body functions were difficult in front of men. Sleeping arrangements were uncomfortable. Men could at least slip away into the open desert in search of privacy. Most women stayed close in, fearing attacks from Iraqi soldiers.

In the end, the message I got from both male and female gulf veterans was: don't rush to judgment on women in combat. Congress should not repeal the exclusion law "until each soldier is home, off leave and able to give her side of the story," says Capt. Gloria Nickerson. Lt. Sandra Nieland, a paratrooper based at Fort Bragg who spent six months in the desert, seconds Nickerson: "The smart way is to research all the problems before Congress acts."

Shoot to kill: It may be that an evaluation of the military's gulf experience will suggest a number of combat roles for women. Any fix will be expensive. It costs $6 million to train an F-16 fighter pilot, for example. If a woman pilot becomes pregnant she doesn't fly. If war comes along, a unit is missing a pilot, and, after the baby, that pilot must requalify. Renovating ship quarters is costly. So is child care and down time to deal with family problems.

There is one last question that can't be answered by further study. The bottom line of war is about killing, and it's unknowable how women will react to this. I spoke to an Army helicopter pilot, Capt. Wendy Mullins at Fort Bragg. Mullins wants to fly the Apache, an awesome tank stalker. Says her instructor pilot, Chief Warrant Officer Ralph Clemons, a veteran of two wars: "She's more than qualified and should be given a shot." When I asked her if she personally could kill, Mullins said: "I accept responsibility that I might shed blood or I may shed the blood of others." The Army has changed. In the old days, the reply would have been, "I'd paint 'em red in a heartbeat." Yet from the look in her warrior eyes and what her male flying mates told me, I have no doubt she'd shoot to kill and win. "There is more trauma hunting deer than tanks," said Mullins. That's true. With standoff weapons, you don't see the tank, only a blip on the scope. Yet later, there's the stress syndrome. Only shrinks and time can tell how the women will cope with the killing that will always be part of the obscenity we call war.

WOMEN HAVE WHAT IT TAKES[4]

Carol Barkalow, 32, born in Clifton Park, N.Y., is a 1980 graduate of West Point. She has commanded an air-defense platoon in Germany and a truck company at Fort Lee, Va., and is author of "In the Men's House," a book about her life in the military. Last week Barkalow spoke with NEWSWEEK's Ginny Carroll at Fort Leavenworth, Kans.:

[4]Article by Ginny Carroll from an interview with Carol Barkalow, in *Newsweek*, Ag 5, 1991, 118:30. ©1991, Carol Barkalow.

I realized I wanted a military career when I was 16, the summer between my junior and senior years of high school. I had been very active in athletics. I enjoyed the discipline, the comradeship, the physicalness of sports, helping other teammates. I also wanted to serve my country. For me, the answer was the Army. My guidance counselor told me that West Point was starting to accept women. I was in the first class.

As plebes, we were required to greet the upperclassmen "Good morning, sir." Too often we'd hear back, "Mornin', bitch." I was naive, I guess. I thought my classmates wanted the same thing I wanted. I thought they would just accept me for that. By the time we graduated, the men's attitudes had begun to mellow somewhat. The women's attitudes had changed, too. If we weren't feminists when we went in, we were when we came out. I went back for my 10-year reunion in October 1990. There was a big difference. My male classmates had changed tremendously. They recognized us as peers. I realized they had been going through their own growth a decade ago, the hell of being a cadet. The reunion was the best time I ever had at West Point.

But some of those old attitudes still linger when the question of women in combat arises. It's a generational issue for the most part. Most of the senior leadership had little opportunity to work with women as peers. Many see us as a mother, a wife, a daughter—especially a daughter. They always say they wouldn't want to see their daughters in combat. What I ask them in return is, would you really want to see your *son* in combat? And isn't it the daughter's choice? One lesson our society learned in the Persian Gulf is that it is no more tragic to lose a mother a sister, a daughter than it is to lose a father, a brother or a son—and no less so.

I volunteered to go to the gulf. I was attached to the 24th Infantry Division, the unit that spearheaded the end-around attack. Our support outfit was in just as much danger as the combat element. The Iraqi weapons had just as much capability of hitting us as the men in front. The difference was that we didn't have the capability to defend ourselves like the combat troops.One question that is always raised is whether women have what it takes to kill an enemy face to face—whether we can handle that particular brand of stress. After my book came out last year, a Vietnam vet named Bill Hanake came to see me. He had a leg and a foot blown off in Vietnam. I think Bill's experience is an eloquent answer to the naysayers who think women don't have what it takes for combat. Both times his unit was overrun in 'Nam, he said, it was the Viet Cong *women* who were the more disciplined, the tougher, who were the most willing to make sure their enemy wasn't going to come back at 'em.

Then there's the argument that men will be overprotective of women. When men are overprotective of *men*, we give them awards for valor. In May, our country awarded an Air Force pilot its second highest medal for leading a nine-hour rescue mission for a fallen flier. That wasn't looked upon as overprotective. Would it have been so if the downed flier had been a woman?

Some believe females would interfere with male bonding. In Saudi, I saw a new type of relationship forming between men and women, one that has traditionally been described among men. It was a nurturing relationship based upon respect, based on sharing the same hardships. The big worry before Vietnam was that blacks couldn't bond with whites. When the bullets started flying, that went away pretty fast. The same type of relationships developed in the gulf between men and women soldiers.

Do I believe women should be allowed to serve in the infantry? Yes, if qualified. The training and physical-strength standards should be uniform. We have standards that we must keep. Our military readiness should never suffer. But I saw a number of physically strong men very scared in Saudi Arabia. It's not just a matter of physical strength. It's mental and emotional strength as well. I think God knew what he was doing when he allowed women to bear the children and gave us the ability to handle that mental and emotional stress.

Pregnancy? The military doesn't have a good handle on the question. When the military looks at pregnancy, it sees it as nonavailability. We had more injuries and nonavailability among men than women in Saudi. Too often, the women are the only ones held responsible for pregnancy, not the men who helped get them that way.

No normal person wants to go into combat. Soldiers are the last people who want to. But we've volunteered. We understand our commitment. Everybody raises a hand, male and female, and swears to support and defend the same Constitution. Women are competent, capable and committed. We are an integral part of the best-trained military force in the world. The services should have the flexibility to assign the best-qualified person to the job, regardless of gender. That's the bottom line.

WOMEN'S WORK[5]

The war is over. The one against Saddam Hussein, at any rate. But another war was fought in the desert, one that continues. Thirty-two thousand troops took part—32,000 female troops. This ongoing war is an emotional one, on all sides. It's a fight for the right to fight.

Women were out there in Desert Storm, on the front lines, in enemy territory. A women led a squadron of Chinook helicopters into Iraq on the first day of the ground war. A woman briefed Gen. Norman Schwarzkopf every night with the latest military intelligence. Women carried M-16s and manned M-60s. They came under fire. They lived like grunts, coping with sand and filth and fear. And they died.

But make no mistake, women were not in combat—at least not as the military technically defines combat. In the Air Force, Navy, and Marines, women are excluded by law from serving in combat, and in the Army they are excluded by policy. Women make up 11 percent of the service. Nevertheless, they are not allowed on fighter planes, aircraft carriers or in any unit with a mission to engage the enemy. They can be on supply ships that travel alongside combat ships; they can fly refueling planes that occupy the same airspace as bombers. They can be on the defensive but not on the offensive.

Offically, keeping women out of combat positions is supposed to reduce their chances of being hurt. But if this high-tech war proved anything, it proved that the traditional concept of the combat zone has been blurred and expanded to include a wide swath of land anywhere within the range of enemy missiles. Three women were among the 28 killed in the Scud attack on Dhahran, 200 miles from the Kuwaiti border. Many women (and men) in the military contend that combat exclusion laws protect women from just one thing: promotions. Lacking battle experience, they cannot pursue a track that could lead to any combat command, from light infantry officer to Chairman of the Joint Chiefs of Staff.

[5]Article by Jeannie Ralston (with reporting by Amy Eskind and Deborah Rawson), from *Life Magazine*, My 1991, 14:52–62. ©1991, *Life Magazine*. Reprinted with permission.

Soon Congress will hold hearings on the role of women in the military. While a woman can attain the highest office of the land—President and Commander-in-Chief—never in the country's 200-year history would she have been able to enter even the lowliest ranks of the infantry. Even though thousands of women risked their lives in Desert Storm, women in the military fear that no one in Congress will be brave enough to stand up for them on this volatile issue and submit a bill that would lift the combat exclusions. They see Capitol Hill as the next theater in their campaign to break into what Congresswoman Pat Schroeder calls "the ultimate tree house—no girls allowed."

At the center of the struggle stand old myths about women and combat, myths that have been repeated with the fervor of all war stories. The women who served in the gulf demolished those myths and replaced them with startling, illuminating realities.

Myth: Women can't perform under pressure.

Thursday, January 21, shortly after midnight. Words come crackling through Lt. Phoebe Jeter's headset, words everyone in Riyadh dreaded: "Scud launch." It is the first time a missile has been lobbed at this capital city, where Jeter, a 27-year old ROTC graduate from Sharon, S.C., who leads a platoon of 15 men, sits in a 21-foot-long Patriot missile control trailer. Hastily putting aside the war novel she has been reading—*Polar Star* by Martin Cruz Smith—Jeter braces for the real thing.

Heart pounding, she stares at a black computer screen. And waits. Waits for the Scuds to show up as upside-down triangles on a blank monitor. A minute, two minutes passs at a glacial pace. "It was just like a vise on my chest," she would say later. Then all at once there are triangles on the screen, the triangles she has to destroy, the triangles she has been trained to destroy in three years of simulated war games.

"Lord, I need to hook it," Jeter mumbles. Superiors constantly tell her she smiles too much, but Jeter is not smiling as she pins the cursor on one of the triangles and calls up data on the system to ascertain the missile's trajectory. The answer: It is headed toward the Riyadh airport and her base. Instantly she gives a command to her tactical control assistant. The assistant pushes a button that fires a Patriot missile. Within moments the triangle on her screen is replaced with a ticktacktoe grid symbol that indicates a hit. One Scud down.

But other triangles crowd the screen. One at a time, Jeter attacks them. As she works, she hears blast after blast as Patriots from another unit hit Scuds directly above her head. Knowing that the Scuds may be carrying chemical warheads, she must strike anything that appears on the screen; even a chunk could have disastrous consequences. Jeter grabs her gas mask and finishes the fight with her face covered in black Butyl rubber.

Then it's over. Debris stops falling, and the all-clear sounds. Jeter strips off her gas mask and sighs. The attack has been beaten off. She ordered 13 Patriots fired and destroyed at least two Scuds. Outside the trailer, members of her unit, Delta Battery, congratulate her on her victory. One pats Jeter on the back, another thanks her for saving his life. Jeter, the first female Scud-buster, a young woman who joined the Army to escape small-town life, proved herself that night in the desert and became the first woman in her battalion to win an Army Commendation Medal. But as far as the Army is concerned, Jeter has not been in combat. Patriots are long-range defensive weapons.

The gulf war was filled with the tales of female soldiers like Jeter who exhibited the right stuff. One sergeant, who served on an elite intelligence gathering team that prepared the way for the beginning of the ground war, was nicknamed the Ice Lady because of her composure in the clutch. Before the Chinook helicopter she flew crashed, Maj. Marie Rossi said, "What I am doing is no greater or less than the man who is flying next to me." Women who perform under pressure invaribly down-play the dangers. Many gave off an I'm-just-doing-my-job attitude; they did not want to be singled out because of their sex, did not want a hint of look-what-Janie-can-do condescension to trivialize their achievements. "I didn't go on the offensive," says Jeter, "but I feel like I have been in combat. I guess the government will acknowledge it in time." Is war a man's game? Says Jeter: "Not anymore."

Myth: Because of sexual tensions and primitive living conditions, the combat zone is no place for a woman

She yanks. She tugs. She catches her breath, then struggles some more. Finally Army Spc. Sandy Hearn a 30-year-old MP, manages to get the 110-pound military rucksack out of the car trunk and onto her back—where it has spent most of the last seven months. One of the many women soldiers who lived like infantrymen during the war, Hearn drove through the Iraqi desert in a convoy for four days to set up the XVIII Airborne Corps's forwardmost POW camp. But that's all over now. With a quick shrug that adjusts the weight on her back, she walks into her house near Fort Bragg, N.C. While she and her two roommates were in Saudi Arabia, the house was broken into and ransacked. But even in its shabby state, it's a palace compared to the living quarters Hearn endured during the war.

On good nights Hearn and three other women slept with 21 men in a tent so cramped that "if anyone turned over you knew it." On other nights she tossed a sleeping bag in the dunes or set up a lean-to on one side of the army vehicle she drove, while her two male team members slept on the other side. Hearn, who saw combat in Panama and has worked as an M-60 gunner, used impromptu desert latrines that were made by parking two jeeps side by side and opening the doors on each vehicle to create a screen of sorts. ("No female will ever go to the front again with out Handi-Wipes," Hearn says.) She went as many as nine days with out a shower.

Today she's back in the States, and it's been 72 hours since she stood under a spigot. She is eager for clean hair and eye shadow, to put on heels and fishnet hose. "It's important to remind yourself that there is a woman in there," says Hearn. In Saudi many "females"—a word the military prefers to "women"—struggled to remind themselves of this while living under grueling conditions. Though more than one soldier wore lace underwear under her fatigues, serious military women are careful never to remind the people they work with of their femininity. "If you do your job, men don't see you as a female, but as a soldier," says Hearn.

Most servicewomen agree that when they act professionally, they are more likely to be treated that way. Outstanding performances can help change the deep-rooted prejudices held by those who oppose women in the military. They can minimize the fear that sexual relations between men and women could compromise a mission, the concern that men would be so protective of a women that they would put themselves in danger unnecessarily.

Certainly there are complications when men and women eat, sleep, work and sweat through danger together. But in many interviews with troops in Saudi Arabia, this much is clear: The problems arising between male and female soldiers are not very different from those encountered by women entering any traditional male territory, be it the locker room or the boardroom. With time and experience, they tend to disappear.

Stereotypes die harder. "When a female is real masculine, yells all the time, men figure she's gay," says Hearn. "If you spend too much time talking to a best buddy, it's going to be the assumption that you slept with him." The lesbian/whore stereotype is an old one for women in the military. Hearn's mother, Sarah, 63, a disabled veteran now confined to a wheelchair, faced it more than 30 years ago. When she joined the Women's Army Corps, her parents almost disowned her. And though she was taught how to pitch a tent in basic training, she was not allowed to sleep in one. Whe she was stationed overseas, she was put up in a hotel.

Clearly, women in the military have come a long way in one generation, but for the younger Hearn they haven't come far enough. She recalls a special training exercise run by Army Rangers that she was qualified to attend but was barred from because there were no "female facilities." Hearn, who will wait to decide whether to reenlist until she finds out what new opportunities are opened to women, is still unhappy that she was unable to attend the exercise. "That excuse will never fly again after Saudi Arabia," she says. "They will never be able to say that they don't have female facilities. Not after what we had to deal with. When you're in a convoy for days and there's no ladies' room and no place to shower, you adapt. It's proven—women have adapted."

There are women, including Hearn, hungry to fight. She joined the MPs in 1988, after six years in the Army, because it was the closest she could get to the infantry. In Panama she escorted convoys, manned lookout posts and came under enemy fire. On the way to her POW camp post in Iraq, she recalls being caught in sandstorm 10 miles behind the fighting. "I have two combat tours, two combat patches," Hearn notes. "I'm one of the few females who can say that." But those experiences are not enough. "It's like hearing about green grass over the hill," Hearn says of the war stories her late father, a drill sergeant, told her when she was growing up. "War is the last male bastion, and I want to see for myself what it's all about."

Myth: Mothers shouldn't—and don't want to—go to war

"You can tear up those letters now," T. Sgt. Cindy Davis whispers to her sister. Her hands—tan from desert sun—rest on the heads of the two children this 32-year-old mother has only been able to dream about since she left Pope Air Force Base in North Carolina last September. She spent those six seemingly endless months on an island in the gulf resupplying cargo planes for the Air Force.

Before the war started in January, Davis wrote letters to her children, Kristen and Tyler, and sent them to her sister with instructions to give them to the kids when they were older if anything should happen to her. "In the letters I said I was sorry I missed football games and proms, and wasn't there on the day they were married." Davis, who has been ecstatic ever since her husband snatched her off the tarmac in a bear hug several hours earlier, suddenly turns solemn and looks down at her children, at Kristen's wide face and dark curls, at Tyler's flushed cheeks. She pulls them closer to her, closer to the green-and-khaki puzzle-piece-pattern fatigues she still wears. "I said I wanted them to be good examples in the world so nothing like this happens again." Davis continues. "I wanted them to know that sometimes you have to fight for something you believe in, and this is something we believed in."

Davis's 30-year-old husband, Jon, an Air Force staff sergeant, believed in the war, too, but he was not called up. "As far as my ego goes, I wish she'd been here and they'd sent me," he says.

But in the kind of role reversal that happened over and over again in this war, it was the man who sent his wife off to war. It was Jon Davis who had to manage the children alone to search for words to explain war to a five-year-old. But it was Cindy Davis who had to endure that heat and the isolation, who hung on to sweet memories of her children's sleeping faces and who pored over snapshots of the people who were waiting for her back home. And it was Cindy Davis who found herself in that painful place of war, that interminable state of not knowing: Would she ever make it back to take her spot in those warm photo album scenes?

"The first month or two was hell," she admits later, sitting on her bed. "But I found that something happened that I was never prepared for: I became detached emotionally. I think that was the only way to survive. I'd get letters about things coming up with my family and I thought, Why don't I feel anything? Why can't I? I was afraid I was losing connection until I realized what was happening." Davis believes other women and men tried to detach themselves as well. She thinks the men were thankful that women were there so they could discuss their longings when they surfaced. "Men won't talk to other men about how they feel about this kind of thing," she says, "but they *will* talk to women. I think having women around make it a little more bearable for men."

The fact that mothers had a positive effect in the gulf was never mentioned in press reports about women being torn from their children to march off to the "Mommy's War." All this made good fodder for politicians, who sponsored bills excusing mothers from deployment. Many military women think that such legislation represents a serious setback in their quest for equal treatment. Nobody likes the idea of any parent—mother or father—being taken away from a family and plunked down in a war zone. But the military is an all-volunteer force, and each single parent or military couple must have a plan worked out for the children's care in case they are shipped out. "When I stayed in the military after I had my children, I accepted that I might have to leave them," says Davis, who left behind her 20-month-old daughter when she went to serve for a year in Italy. "And I'd go again."

Though Davis personally does not want to serve on the front line, she doesn't question her ability to do so. "I could shoot someone if I put in my mind why I was doing it—for my children. I was over there to protect my children, to make sure that they grow up in a free country."

Myth: The public isn't ready for female POWs or women in body bags

The funeral was over when they finally talked about it. Sgt. Cheryl LaBeau-O'Brien's body had made the trip from Saudi Arabia to Dover Air Force Base to the Northwest cargo terminal in Milwaukee to the Purath-Strand Funeral Home in her hometown of Racine, Wis. And ultimately to the cemetery up on a small knoll, where there had been nothing to stop the wind. And nothing to stop the family's grief over losing a 24-year-old daughter in a war that had once seemed so distant, but now seemed too close.

Her parents' house is filled with floral arrangements. And with emotions: sadness, anger, despair, guilt for things left undone. And with memories: memories of a woman who loved her job servicing aircraft for the Army's 1st Infantry and was proud to go to the gulf in January along with her husband, Michael. The house is also filled with people who take some consolation in knowing that this woman had said before her Black Hawk helicopter was shot down near the Iraqi border that if she died, she'd die happy.

"You know, I didn't believe there was a place in the military for women," says Cheryl's father, Bill LaBeau, who like his daughter was an aircraft technician, but for the Navy. "We argued about this many times." But now Bill has changed his mind. "It has been proven to me that women do their job and they do it damn well. Watching television reports of this war made me understand this."

"But the ultimate proof was your daughter," says Cheryl's mother, Lois.

"Men have the upper hand when it comes to physical strength," says Michael O'Brien, a sergeant who was stationed two miles away from Cheryl in the desert. "But when it comes to ability, it doesn't matter—male or female. I don't want to see anyone die in battle. But it's a woman's right to do what she wants to do."

"Yes," her father acknowledges. "She made the ultimate sacrifice."

Cheryl LaBeau-O'Brien was one of 10 women killed after the fighting began on Janaury 16. Her death was especially painful because she was killed following the cease-fire at the hands of Iraqi troops who didn't know the war was over. Her new husband had been thanking God that they'd made it through the war when he was called in to see his commanding officer. He took one look at the chaplain sitting next to him and knew his thanks had been premature.

Is the death of Cheryl LaBeau-O'Brien more tragic because she was a woman? Few now would say so. The idea that one life is more valuable than another insults both sexes; it diminishes all people.

"There hasn't been any national hue and cry over the deaths of the women," admits Rep. Beverly Byron, who chairs the congressional subcommittee that will study women in the military. At the memorial service for those killed in the Scud attack, the governor of Pennsylvania described two of the victims as "a former high school football star and a future homemaker of America." But the mourners, like death itself, did not discriminate: There were tears for all.

And the public remained composed though anxious when two women were held as POWs. After they were released, fears that they might have been raped and seriously abused proved unfounded.

"I think after this war, the body bag issue can be put to rest," says Carolyn Becraft, military consultant for the Women's Research and Education Institute. It's a difficult one to put away, though, because death is inevitably surrounded by wrenching "what-ifs," "whys" and "if onlys."

At the LaBeau house, the family tries to maintain perspective, to keep in mind that Cheryl was doing what she wanted to do. "People used to tell me not to worry, that Cheryl would be many miles back," says Lois LaBeau. "I know how committed she was, and I used to tell people that with what Cheryl was doing, she was bound to be close to the front lines. I knew that if something needed to be done, she would never say, 'No, I'm not going. That's combat zone.' She wouldn't think of it."

"Cheryl wouldn't have said, 'Let it be a man,'" Michael says quietly. "Cheryl would have said, 'Let it be me.'"

WHAT'S WRONG WITH THE NAVY?[6]

A curious ethnological specimen, the U.S. Naval officer is developing artificially in the direction of sleekness and culture. . . . The world, pondering on the great part of its own future, which is in his hands, contemplates him with wonder as to what the devil he will evolve into in another century or two.

—George Bernard Shaw, 1899

Not quite a century after Shaw's uncertain observation, the USS Saratoga hovers within a day's steaming time of the wreck-

[6]Excerpted from article by Peter Cary and Bruce B. Auster from *U.S. News & World Report*, Jl 13, 1992. ©July, 13, 1992, *U.S. News & World Report*. Reprinted with permission.

age of Yugoslavia, prepared to project American force once again into a dangerous and distant part of the world. It would seem a reassuring image to a nation still attempting to come to grips with its status as a superpower in a unipolar world—except that the Navy today is an institution in profound crisis.

At a moment when the service is confronted with some of the most far-reaching questions in its history, Navy brass find themselves reeling from a series of embarrassing tactical failures and cover-ups of flawed investigations. The most recent stain on the handsome Navy shield is a scandal that includes sexual misconduct by drunken and abusive aviators and a leadership that, until long after it was too late, seemed to see nothing amiss in its prvileged ranks. Incredibly, coming hard on the heels of the notorious Tailhook scandal last week [July , 1992], two Navy aviators were disciplined for hanging a banner inside the officers' club at the famous Top Gun training base that made a lewd reference to Colorado Rep. Patricia Schroeder, an influential member of the House Armed Services Committee. "The times have changed," Adm. Frank Kelso, the chief of naval operations, vowed in an interview. "We have to change with them."

New missions. Change has never come easily for the Navy, however. Indeed, as ugly as it was, the Tailhook scandal that has forced the resignation of Navy Secretary H. Lawrence Garrett might be considered just another Pentagon contretemps were it not for the light it shines on a culture and a uniformed leadership singularly unable, among America's military services, to come to terms with the new rules of a more inclusive society.

The Navy also is struggling to adapt in the post-cold-war world. In the bad old days, it was the Air Force and the Army at the forefront in stopping a Soviet nuclear attack or an armored thrust at the heart of Central Europe. Today, as the war along the Dalmatian Coast demonstrates, it is the Navy more than ever before that will be called upon to project American force where needed. Navy brass, even according to some in the Pentagon, seem dizzied by the sudden new challenges. "They are so wedded to old roles and missions, to the stovepipe culture and how to get their next star," says one senior defense official, "that they are incapable of realizing what this country needs in its Navy."

It is not just the latest scandal that bedevils the Navy, however. In the past decade, despite its sterling accomplishments in antisubmarine warfare and in fielding a credible strategic nuclear deterrent, the Navy's performance has been spotty when it has been called upon to deliver force far away from American shores. Successes have been offset by failures from Grenada to the mistaken shooting down of an Iranian airbus with 290 in the Persian Gulf. The record is especially alarming because even some Navy planners now recognize that the role of the service must change, and change drastically.

A major strategic review, called the Naval Force Capabilities Planning Effort, observes that almost all military conflicts since World War II have been fought within 200 miles of shore. Noting that these littoral areas are well within the range of Navy tactical aircraft flying from carriers, the study's authors emphasized the benefits of a smaller "brown water" fleet, a far cry from the world-girding "blue water" force the Navy and nation have historically prided themselves on. But the study, still unreleased, was almost never completed. Last year, Navy Secretary Garrett told the chief of naval operations and the commandant of the Marine Corps to start over and rethink the Navy's role in U.S. military strategy. However, the Navy's top uniformed leadership ignored the secretary's directive. Finally, a handful of officials bypassed the bureaucracy and completed the white paper themselves.

This is the same culture from which Tailhook was born. It is a culture that has been both intent on its privileges and intolerant of interference from outsiders, whether they be colleagues from other services, congressional oversight committees or even contractors questioning bizarre procurement practices. The service of the Kennedys, the Roosevelts and the Bushes, the Navy has long been a bastion of elitism. It was a service in which the privileged lived comfortably in "officer country," sleeping in staterooms on clean sheets and waited on by black and Filipino mess stewards.

Rum and the lash. More to the point, perhaps, because of its legacy from the British Navy and the demands of an infant nation, the Navy evolved differently than the other military services. The Constitution, for instance, allowed for a permanent Navy but provided for the raising of armies only in times of emergency. Soldiers, not sailors, were expected to return to their farms after the threat of war had passed. It was the Navy, not the Army, that kept an isolated and isolationist country safe by controlling its oceans.

Perhaps most of all, it is because of the peculair traditions of the sea that the Navy is such a breed apart. Life is different aboard a ship. Winston Churchill, when he was Britain's First Lord of the Admiralty, sneered at the three time-honored traditions of the Royal Navy, "rum, sodomy and the lash." Sailors today routinely spend three to six months at a time at sea, compared with the yearlong cruises of ages past. Still, the insularity of shipboard life is not unlike that of the sailors of yore celebrated by Shaw, Samuel Eliot Morrison and Alfred Thayer Mahan. The demands are constant. "The Navy is different in that it is constantly operating," says James Webb, a Vietnam veteran and former Navy secretary. "There is very little difference in what they do between peacetime and wartime." Ship captains have power over their sailors that Army officers haven't over troops. The captain decides whether the crew gets hard-tack and when to put ashore for fresh water. "You can't go AWOL on a ship," says one officer. "You can only jump overboard and die."

The captain's prerogative bred arrogance—and it has thrived in the Navy to this day. "There's an ultimate arrogance. They believe they're above examination, that their judgment is not to be questioned," says Tom Hahn, a former Navy scientist and House Armed Services Committee lawyer. Adds another congressional aide: "We called it the goddam Navy, the arrogant Navy. It emanates from the fact that in that culture they get command of the ship and everybody bows to them."

The Navy is not a monolith, however. Within the service, two breeds, aviators and submariners, are at the top of the pecking order. Lately, aviators have dominated. It is emblematic, therefore, that the scandal that has thrust the Navy into its current harsh light is named Tailhook. To land on a pitching aircraft carrier deck, a pilot must catch a thick metal cable with his plane's tailhook. "A Navy pilot won't care how many bombs he's dropped, but he can tell you the exact number of landings he's made on a carrier," says one officer. "It's the most important thing, catching that wire. It's what gives them their swagger."

Rowdy behavior That swagger seems to be what gets so many Navy aviators in trouble on solid ground. "You have to be a little bit crazy to fly airplanes off ships," says Charles Moskos of Northwestern University, an expert on the culture of the military. "If you get too civilized, you iron out the atavistic behavior that makes a good pilot."

Some of those pilots clearly crossed the line last fall at the annual convention of the Tailhook Association at the Las Vegas Hilton. Junior officers sexually assaulted fellow officers, including an admiral's aide, Lt. Paula Coughlin, who publicly described the attack on her by several officers. The scandal, which escalated when the Naval Investigative Service failed to get to the bottom of the incident during a months-long inquiry, has led to the resignation of Secretary Garrett, who had attended the convention and apparently had a beer on the patio adjoining a room where drunken aviators hosted parties with strippers and prostitutes. (Garrett has said he did not know what was happening inside.) The incident has also led to investigations by the Pentagon's inspector general and by the House Armed Services Committee.

What happened inside the Tailhook convention surprised few fliers, however. One naval aviator from Virginia Beach who asked not to be named says that rowdy behavior is the rule at his squadron's bachelor parties. He said that aviators typically hired strippers and prostitutes. By night's end, the women may have given the feted bachelor oral sex and serviced a bunch of his buddies as well. "That kind of stuff is not only tolerated," the aviator says, "it's halfway encouraged." He said his squadron's executive officer recently lectured them on their bachelor parties. The problem? Squadron wives were finding out about the wild times.

Tailhook, at bottom, then, was not just a failure of culture but of leadership. At a symposium at the convention, for example, aviators were given the chance to address questions to the Navy's top officers. During one session, a number of aviators in the audience who opposed allowing women to fly in combat wore buttons that read "Not in my Squadron." The Navy's assistant chief of naval operations for air warfare, Vice Adm. Richard Dunleavy, was a member of the panel. Assigned to field questions from the floor, he smilingly wore a button with a target on it. When a woman asked Dunleavy when women would be allowed to fly in combat, the admiral ducked under a table. The audience laughed.

"It wasn't just the boys acting like juveniles," says a top Pentagon official. "It was the leadership." Admiral Kelso, the chief of naval operations, was in the audience. He says he did not see the buttons but believes now that those aviators should have been forced to remove them. Sen. Bob Kerry, a Democrat from Nebraska who served in the Navy during Vietnam and lost part of a leg, fumes over the incident: "I believe there is a great power in having just one person shout *No!* as loud as hell in the midst of a room full of people going in the other direction."

If the Navy is to right itself after Tailhook, it will take forceful new leadership. In a caustic speech to some 300 senior officers at the Pentagon last week, Acting Navy Secretary Dan Howard sought to turn the tide. He has proposed amending military law to make sexual harassment a crime. For serious offenses, such as sexual assault, a sailor would automatically be discharged. Other efforts are underway. The Navy has instituted a series of courses, which it calls a program of core values, to educate its sailors about sexual harassment. "There's a subculture here," Howard told *U.S. News* last week, "the macho man idea, the hard drinking, skirt chasing that goes with the image of the Navy and Marines. That crap's got to go."

Race and sex The Navy has managed change of this kind before. Adm. Elmo Zumwalt, who was chief of naval operations from 1970 to 1974, fought an entrenched Navy in order to integrate it racially. From World War II to the 1950s, blacks and Filipinos could serve in the Navy—but only as stewards. Half of the Navy's blacks were still in the steward service when other services began to desegregate. "There is an irony here," says Edwin Dorn, a former Army officer and civil-rights expert at Brookings Institution. "The Navy was the first sevice to adopt [a policy of] racial integration but the last to implement it."

To prevail, Zumwalt had to take on the Navy culture and change it. "We concluded," he says, "that we had to put every person in the Navy through sensitivity training on race relations." Only after special recruiting efforts did the Navy by the late 1980s reach rough parity with the other services in terms of minority representation.

Integrating the Navy sexually, however, could be significantly more difficult. For reasons of morale, it may be impractical to integrate women into every aspect of Navy life. In the close quarters of a submarine, for example, the problems of sexual fraternization might be insurmountable. But that is different from training Navy men to accept women as a force in the force. "I found it easier to persuade a senior naval officer to treat a black man as his equal," Zumwalt says, "than it was to persuade him to treat a woman as an equal in the military profession."...

Inside the Tailhook Affair

Nearly a year after 26 women reported attacks and assorted violent sexual assaults during a convention of Navy aviators last September, no criminal charges have been brought. Pentagon inspectors say they are still trying to establish what happened at the "Tailhook '91 Symposium." They say that criminal charges may yet be brought. A review of a 2,200-page declassified investigative document on the Tailhook incident paints a frightening picture of drunken and abusive Navy officers who manhandled, bit and disrobed women officers and civilians as they attempted to traverse the third-floor corridor of the Las Vegas Hilton, a ritual Tailhook members refer to as "running the gantlet." Excerpts:

• "The third-floor hallway was . . . crowded with Navy and Marine Corps pilots, most of whom had been drinking. The gantlet [involved] bumping, pushing, touching and rubbing women as they walked through the hallway. . . . Hand and verbal signs were used to identify those women deemed attractive enough to be subjected to the gantlet."

• A woman officer told how "one male grabbed her buttocks with both hands. He then moved behind her, pressing his pelvis to her buttocks as he moved her down the hallway. . . . This individual placed both of his hands down her shirt and bra, grabbing both her breasts. In an attempt to escape his grasp, [the woman officer] crouched over and grabbed his wrists, biting his left forearm and then his right hand between the thumb and forefinger. The assault continued as other members of the gantlet grabbed her breasts and buttocks. One individual reached under her skirt and grabbed her panties, apparently in an attempt to remove them. Her attempt to escape the gantlet through an open door of a hospitality suite was blocked by two males. . . . [The woman officer] solicited another unknown male to help her. He responded by grabbing her breasts."

• A male officer attending his first Tailhook convention described the gantlet: "Sometimes clusters of women would pass through with only a few of them taking exception to the activity . . . [although] two women slapped an assailant or pushed one away. At this time, the activity appeared quite harmless . . . .[Then] a young female who was extremely intoxicated came out of a suite and entered the gantlet. As she went through the gantlet, a pair of pants popped out of the top of the group. The young female collapsed on the floor, and within seconds the gantlet dispersed, leaving her on the floor. Two security guards moved in at this time, picked her up and removed her from the hallway. She was wearing only a shirt and pantyhose at this time."

• A woman member of the Tailhook Association told investigators she was assaulted repeatedly by a Navy officer: "[The officer] bit her on the buttocks . . . and she told him he was out of line. Later on, while conversing with other individuals, the aforementioned suspect approached her from behind and bit her once again on the buttocks. Several individuals came to her aid, including a security officer who escorted the suspect off the hotel floor. . . . [Later], while visiting the third floor of the Hilton with a friend, [the woman officer] was bitten on the hip by a Caucasian male with sandy brown hair cut in military style." The following night, the woman's original assailant returned to the Tailhook gathering and "bit her buttocks, [and she] turned and kicked her assailant, who quickly departed the area."

• Another woman officer, who told investigators she was "practically gang-banged by a group of F-18 pilots" crowded into the hotel's third-floor corridor, complained to her commanding officer two weeks after the convention: "I said, 'Sir, I don't think you understand how bad that thing was in Tailhook. It was the worst thing that ever happened to me'. . . . [A fellow officer, a male] was walking by my desk, and upon overhearing my remarks, stated, 'That's what you get when you go to a hotel party with a bunch of drunk aviators.'"

THE HOMEFRONT REACTION

EDITOR'S INTRODUCTION

The final section presents various and conflicting assessments of what has been achieved by having women serve in the military.

The opening article in this section, written by Melinda Beck in *Newsweek*, examines the duty and danger in a "Mom's War." Servicewomen's involvement in the Iraqi invasion is discussed, as well as the effect female casualties will have on the ongoing debate.

The next three articles appeared in *The National Review*. The first, by William F. Buckley Jr., asks readers whether the role of women in combat does indeed reflect "a civilized order." Mr. Buckley maintains that the question is not about women's rights but rather about the order of nature. In the second article, Elaine Donnelly writes that women "sharing a field tent with men learn some facts of life the ideologues don't know" and suggests that the Gulf War was a failure for feminists, whose "most cherished theories . . . crumbled in the face of fundamental realities of human nature." The last of the three articles, by Florence King, deals with feminist demands and their effect on the nation.

Next, Anne Summers writing for *Ms.*, reflects on Congresswoman Pat Schroeder's views and the opposition she has met while supporting women's involvement in the armed forces. In order to assure a place for women in the future military, Schroeder is committed to adjusting standing rules and regulations and taking the flak from wherever it may come. The sixth article, by Jean Bethke Elshtain, is aptly titled "Feminism and War", and discusses these two strange bedfellows. The article also explores the "Gulf Orphan" problem, the plight of children whose parents were called to duty, who blame "themselves for their parents' absence. . . . "

In the seventh article, reprinted from *Time*, Julie Johnson writes of the Senate's measure to "allow but not require each of the services to certify women pilots for combat missions," and the formation of a White House-chosen panel to report on the issue of women in combat [Fall 1992]. The eight article by Richette L. Haywood, reprinted from *Jet* magazine, describes the effects women serving overseas has on the families they leave behind and how those families cope.

In the final article of this compilation, reprinted from *The New York Times*, Linda Bird Francke writes of a female soldier's funeral that causes the author to reflect not only as an American but also as a mother of daughters who are old enough to enlist, on the role of women in the military.

OUR WOMEN IN THE DESERT[1]

The troops in Saudi Arabia have given this crisis a nickname: the "mom's war." The evidence is everywhere in the heat and dust. Maj. Kathy Higgins pinned up a crayon drawing by her 5 year-old son in her medical evacuation office. A few U.S. servicewomen have torn up photos of their children; looking at them was just too hard. Sitting in a field hospital on the edge of a bustling airstrip, Lt. Col. Carolyn Roaf, a medical officer, said that saying goodbye to her 6-year-old daughter was the toughest thing she had ever done—especially after the little girl told her, "Mom, if you die over there, I'm coming to rescue you." Capt. Ginny Thomas left the Air Force three years ago because she wanted more of a home life. Last week she was back as a reservist, piloting a giant C-141 transport around the Middle East. "I'll be glad when it's over," she said. "But I would be disappointed if I was not over here doing something for my country."

Women have taken part in every American military crisis since the Revolutionary War. But never before have they served on such a large scale or in such a wide variety of jobs. As the massive deployment in the Persian Gulf continues, women pilots from the 101st Airborne Division are ferrying supplies and personnel in Huey helicopters. Female mechanics from the 24th Mechanized Division are maintaining tanks, handling petroleum and coordinating water supply. Throughout the region, women

[1]Article by Melinda Beck, from *Newsweek*, S 10, 1990, 116:22-5. ©1990, Newsweek, Inc. Reprinted by permission.

are working as truck drivers, cargo handlers, intelligence specialists, paratroopers, flight controllers, shipboard navigators, communications experts and ground-crew chiefs. Their precise number in Operation Desert Shield is classified but one Army personnel expert says women will soon match their overall proportion in the services: roughly 11 percent of the 2 million-member armed forces.

Women are still not permitted to serve in combat positions—by law in the Navy, Air Force and Marines and by policy in the Army. But ever since the Pentagon began recruiting women in large numbers in the 1970s . . . , the services have defined "combat" ever more narrowly, giving women increasingly critical roles. That has caused some confusion in past deployments. In the invasion of Grenada, four female MPs were stopped at the loading ramp and sent back to their barracks three times while the brass hashed out its policy. This time there was no holding back, the Pentagon said: if women were part of a unit stateside, they shipped out when it was deployed. Only the Marine Corps showed some hesitancy, deliberately delaying a few support units that contained women in the early days of the mobilization. But a Camp Pendleton spokeswoman denied reports that men had actually been substituted for women, and since then, the Marines, too, have sent women to the gulf.

For now, the U.S. servicewomen in Saudi Arabia are doing just what the men are doing: setting up vast military installations in the desert, fortifying supply lines and waiting. If the shooting begins, there are no plans to withdraw the women from the theater and few illusions that they might not be among the casualties. "Just because you're not in a combat unit doesn't mean you won't be in combat," says Lawrence Korb, former assistant secretary of Defense for manpower. "When they start lobbing SCUDS with chemical weapons, they'll be aiming at everybody." To that end, female troops in Saudi Arabia have been issued protective gear, and are required to carry it at all times, just like the men. They also carry arms and are trained to use them should they come under attack.

Harm's Way: Some military experts say the gulf call-up underscores the hypocrisy of Pentagon policies toward women: though they can't serve on the fighting lines, they are in harm's way—particularly in a conflict where the "frontline" could be everywhere. "Every military manual instructs you to hit the back supplyline first and try to isolate the front line," says Rep. Patricia Schroeder, who chairs the House subcommittee on military installations. "Where are all the women? In the back lines with the supply details, communications equipment and refueling planes."

Given the desert realities, some service women are lobbying the military to lift the combat restrictions. "I can fly that F-15 just as well as a man," insists 25-year-old Lt. Stephanie Shaw, who controls flight missions for a tactical air wing in the gulf. "I volunteered for the Army, not the Girl Scouts," echoes Capt. Leola Davis, commander of a heavy-maintenance company that fixes everything from tanks to HUMV jeeps at the Army's First Cavalry Division at Fort Hood, Texas. But the objections to women on the front lines are deeply entrenched, as Schroeder found this year when she proposed legislation calling for a four-year Army test of women in combat posts. The Army rejected the idea, and it stands little chance of passage.

One of the chief arguments against women on the fighting lines is sheer physical strength. Within the tough, tattooed all-male tanker brigades at Fort Hood, for example, it's an article of faith that women don't have the upper body strength to load 60-pound shells into guns. But brute force is irrelevent in many of the combat jobs from which women are excluded. "On a ship, war is high tech," says one former Navy submariner. "Men aren't any better at video games than women."

Male Bonding: Many military men firmly believe the presence of women on the front lines would disrupt what they call "unit cohesion"—the male bonding that theoretically allows warriors to perform acts of heroism under fire. "I want people on my right and on my left who will take the pressure when the shooting starts," says Brig. Gen. Ed Scholes, who commands the 18th Airborne Corps in Saudi Arabia. "Men simply cannot treat women like other men. And it's silly to think that a few month's training can make them into some kind of sexless soldiers," says Brian Mitchell, a former Army captain and author of a 1989 book, "Weak Link: The Feminization of the American Military." But historian Linda Grant De Pauw, founder of the Minerva Center, which studies women in the military, counters that such objections are mired in old stereotypes of women as victims. "It's like the image they used to have of blacks before they served with them—that they were too cowardly, too stupid or would break their weapons," she argues.

Justified or not, the restrictions have created a military rife with anomalies. Women can train men for missions they can't carry out themselves. In some cases, they can command units in which they can't serve. Air Force women can ferry troops and supplies over hostile areas, and refuel jet fighters, but they can't fly the fighters. In the Navy, they are barred from permanent assignment on combat ships such as carriers, destroyers and submarines. But they can serve on repair and supply ships in the same waters. In 1987, 248 women were aboard the destroyer tender Acadia, which came to the aid of the USS Stark after it was hit by an Iraqi Exocet missile. Women also make up a quarter of the firefighters on the sub tender USS Dixon. "If you have women fighting a fire in an enclosed area, that's just as dangerous as a combat zone," says reservist Teresa Smith, a first class petty officer who would report to the Dixon if called to active duty.

'Glass Ceiling': What's more, servicewomen say the restrictions hamper their career opportunities. Army officials boast that 285 of the 331 "military occupational specialties" are open to enlisted women. But in fact, only half the jobs in noncombat specialties are available to women, since some are in tank, infantry or other units that are off-limits. Women officers also bitterly complain that the rules have created a "glass ceiling," since advancement to top ranks often depends on leading combat units. "A number of women say, 'Hey, don't protect me from combat' because the price is too high," says Navy Capt. Susan Canfield, who oversees nine ships mapping the Pacific for antisubmarine warfare.

The lust for more action is not universally shared among U.S. servicewomen, however. At Fort Hood, Chief Warrant Officer 2 Portia Dublar, a crack maintenance technician for the Second Armored Division's aviation brigade, says she has no burning desire to fly helicopters—"I'm perfectly content to fix them." Sgt. Elizabeth Hope, one of the few women deployed in Saudi Arabia who has seen combat before as an MP in Panama, thinks women should not serve in the trenches: "It would simply complicate everything if women were fighting alongside men."

Ultimately, the decision to allow more women in combat, at least in the Navy, Marines and Air Force, rests with Congress, where opposition is most deeply entrenched of all. Much of that stems from the perception that the U.S. public won't stomach its daughters coming home in body bags. Yet historian D'Ann Campbell, teaching at West Point, notes that "women have *always* come back in body bags. The question is, are we going to train them for defense? It will depend on how essential it is for the military to be all it can be."

The U.S. women in Saudi Arabia face a more immediate problem—the clash of cultures with their Muslim hosts. In a country where women can't drive, show their faces or venture out alone, Saudi troops don't know what to make of female GIs wearing fatigues and issuing orders. American women are similarly stunned by the Saudis. Two female paratroopers, interviewed in Dhahran last week, couldn't help but stare as a Muslim woman in a black veil walked by. "Tragic," said First Lt. Jennifer Ann Wood, who quoted a maxim from her West Point days: "That's a tradition unhampered by progress."

The Saudis have made some cultural concessions. U.S. servicewomen can now discreetly drive vehicles while on duty, and at one air base, they can use a gym during limited hours, though they must enter through the back door. Still, they are not permitted to wear shorts, jog or even shop on military bases unless accompanied by a man. Some American women take the restrictions in stride: "This is their culture. We shouldn't impose our ways on them," said Capt. Susan Beausoleil, a paratrooper with the 18th Airborne Corps. Others aren't so complacent. The Saudis "look at you like a dog—they don't want American women here," griped one Army staff sergeant. That kind of treatment incenses Schroeder, as does the U.S. military's tolerance. "Can you imagine if we sent black soldiers to South Africa and told them to go along with the apartheid rules?" she asks.

Limited Comforts: Conditions could be worse for the U.S. women. Many are quartered in air-conditioned barracks, mobile homes and schools built by the Saudis. All-male Marine combat units deployed further forward live in sweltering tents without cold drinks or hot meals. Even in rear areas, though, comforts are limited. Women often sleep 24 to a room, on cots only three inches apart. There are occasional shortages of such essentials as sanitary napkins. With nowhere to go after hours, no movies or recreational facilities, boredom sets in quickly. Many women just work, sleep and do laundry. Deprived of TV, some have rediscovered the pleasures of reading and the art of conversation.

Much of the talk is of spouses and children. Military rules specify that single parents and two-career service couples must designate short- and long-term guardians for their dependents. But most servicewomen never thought such arrangements would actually be used, and the reality is heart wrenching. Sgt. Mary Payette, an antitank weapons specialist, left her 8-month-old son with her sister in St. Paul and can't help but think what would happen if she didn't return. She shudders: "I don't want him calling anybody else Mom."

Some U.S. military women are also married to military men, and fear for their safety. Army ordnance specialist Karen Norrington arrived in Saudi Arabia to discover that her husband had been shipped over, too, in a different unit. "I've stayed out here looking for him," she said, as she scanned the ranks of arriving soldiers at a Saudi receiving point. Kim and Robert Williams of Flint, Mich., were luckier. They were stationed together to the Persian Gulf. "We're having fun," said Kim, though she added that the worst part is not knowing how long they will be away. "We could be here for a few weeks or a year. Maybe our children won't remember us."

The U.S. women in Saudi Arabia joined the armed forces for much the same reasons men have flocked to the colors—excitement, travel, patriotism and a chance for skills they couldn't get elsewhere. But many didn't plan on this kind of adventure. Just like the men, they are scared—of the strange, forbidding desert, of an unpredictable enemy and especially the threat of a poison-gas attack. "Anyone who says he or she is not scared is lying to themselves," says Lt. Stephanie Shaw. "I wake up each morning hoping my arrival in Saudi Arabia was just a dream," admits Army specialist Sandra Chisholm. "But we have a job to do here and we will do it."

No one can predict what that job will ultimately entail for the American troops. But the women, more than the men, believe their future in the armed forces is on the line that George Bush has drawn in the sand. If a major war erupts, spreading unisex casualties throughout the theater, it could finally bring down the combat exclusions—or it could so outrage the American public, and its leaders, that women are never again placed so close to the action in so many critical roles.

MILITARIZE WOMEN?[2]

The Senate has now passed a bill permitting women who volunteer to fly combat aircraft to do so, and the movement to extend the rights of women to equality in the trenches is growing. Give a thought, please, to this demurral.

1. The practical arguments, in favor and against, have occupied most of the time of the jurists brought in to decide the question. It is observed that, on average, men are 40 per cent stronger than women. Does that sound decisive to you? Perhaps, in which case you have given the subject insufficient thought, for the simple reason that there is little correlation between human strength and military skill. This is not to say that there are no situations in which sheer brute physical force isn't critically useful, but such situations are put in place by recalling that Napoleon was 5 feet 3, and that T. E. Lawrence weighed less than 150 pounds.

2. A corollary of the above is the argument that women's reflexes are every bit as fast as men's and that success or failure as a modern soldier, particularly in a fighter aircraft, depends on the speed of reponse. If Amy can read the dials and do the correct thing just as fast as Roger, why should the Air Force discriminate against her? The answer of course is that the Air Force should not discriminate against her, if speed of response is the only criterion relevant.

3. To the argument that in combat conditions it is a burden to provide two sets of washroom facilities, the pleaders for what they call women's rights argue to the effect that in combat situations, antimacassar niceties become simply irrelevant. Both men and women go up in spacecraft, and mixed company have made long passages, on small boats and even on rafts. Primitive cultures simply ignore biological differences at this level, and war-making has a great deal to learn from primitive cultures, where the objective is the thing that rules, not the taboo, which is properly relegated to insignificance.

Very well then, the arguments in favor of women in the military are in. Here is the side to which I belong:

[2]Article by William F. Buckley Jr., from his *On the Right* Column, from *The National Review*, S 9, 1991, 43:54. ©1991, Universal Press Syndicate. Reprinted with permission.

1. The attempt to equalize the sexes is going to be asymptotic. You think you have reached equality, but there is still a tiny difference there. That difference bespeaks an insight which is a hallmark of civilization.

2. It is a pity that the useless word "equality" ever got into the act, because one cannot in the nature of things make "equal" that which is not the same. You can play around with other words if you wish. Fungible? No, the sexes aren't fungible. Miscible? Yes: but miscible elements retain their identity. If the sexes weren't miscible, life together would be impossible.

The point is that men and women are different, and that it is *of nature (ex natura)* that one sex should be drawn to one pursuit (among many), the other to another pursuit (among many). That a woman should aspire to be a poet or an architect, a doctor or an engineer, does no violation to the critical insight of separateness of nature. But that a woman should ignore that which binds her to the newborn child or enjoins her to comfort men who cannot adequately be comforted by other men is a tug against nature. And that a man, himself a poet or a doctor or an engineer or an architect, should cease instinctively to gravitate to his responsibility to protect the home is—a violation of his nature.

The awful, fanatical compulsion to perfect interchangeable sexes does violence to primary instincts that are wrong when abused, as they were singularly abused when, for instance, women were not allowed even to vote. But to overcorrect an abuse is to commit a fresh abuse. Because we know that women should be educated and should vote and should exercise their capacity to lead does not dissipate that tropism that assigns to the woman primary responsibility for the care of the child, and to the man, primary responsibility for the care of the woman.

Transplanting it all onto the battle scene we need to wonder whether the machine gunner exposing his life to effect a mission isn't dismayed at the thought of a young woman firing away at his side, causing him to wonder, wonder, whether the fight he is fighting reflects a civilized order.

"WHAT DID YOU DO IN THE GULF, MOMMY?"[3]

The Gulf War, universally abhorred by feminist ideologues, served nonetheless as a vehicle to put into practice their most cherished theories. With relentless efficiency, the Pentagon tested the hypothesis that in a unisex world, men and women are interchangeable in all occupations—that it makes no difference who does the soldiering and who does the mothering.

But the experiment was not a success. As it stretched from weeks into months, feminist theories began to crumble in the face of fundamental realities of human nature. The nation was traumatized, for example, by the sight of babies being left behind by helmeted young mothers on their way to the Gulf. Pictures of male soldiers leaving their children behind have always tugged at the heart, but there was an extra dimension of uneasiness because of the number of single mothers and of couples who were both in the service. In a recent *Newsweek* poll 89 per cent of respondents said they are still troubled by the the idea of mothers going to war.

Then there were the sexual tensions that did not respond to bureaucratic mandates for professionalism in the workplace. In spite of Pentagon management of the news, there were many reports of illegal fraternization, genuine sexual harassment, and elevated pregnancy rates—all of which seriously affected readiness and morale.

These problems cannot be blamed on women alone, or on men as a group. Rather, they were due to unrealistic expectations for a unisex world which do not allow for human characteristics, normal emotions, and personal weaknesses.

Disappearing Feminists

When the going got rough in Saudi Arabia, feminists who wring their hands about sexual harrassment in the workplace

[3]Article by Elaine Donnelly, a former member of the Defense Advisory Committee on Women in the Services (DACOWITS) and Executive Director of the Coalition for Military Readiness. From *The National Review*, N 18, 1991, 43:41-4. © 1991, *The National Review*, Inc. Reprinted by permission.

were nowhere to be found. While criticizing Middle Eastern society for not allowing women to drive cars, they ignored the plight of enlisted women who had to put up with little or no privacy in co-ed field tents, makeshift showers, unsanitary latrines, and the constant companionship of men equipped with military-issue condoms that were not intended for the women swathed in veils.

But of course feminist leaders rarely denounce conditions that they insist *other* women can endure. In 1989, Canadian Assitant Defense Minister Mary Collins reportedly commented that sexual incidents in the field may be "the price of equality" for military women.

Civilian feminists consistently make inconsistent demands in the name of miltary women. When it comes to co-ed field tents and mothers going to war, they insist on strict equality. But when it comes to physical requirements that are directly related to the job, they insist on double standards.

During Senate hearings in June on the issue of women in combat, members of the Armed Services Committee heard a great deal of testimony about "gender-norming"—the practice of routinely scoring women's physical test results differently from men's. When I visited West Point in 1985, I noticed, for example, that a female cadet's "A" performance on the obstacle course was the same as that graded "C" for a man. Gender-norming is designed to fudge the truth that everyone knows: on average, women are not as physically strong as men. Faced with this inconvenient truth, the Pentagon has made "adjustments" for women.

In 1982, for example, the Women in the Army (WITA) project was to match individual physical capabilities to the demands of Army Jobs. But the Pentagon based Defense Advisory Committee on Women in the Services (DACOWIT) complained that sex-neutral standards to qualify recruits were unfair because they tended to disqualify women.

The Pentagon promptly gave in on the point and downgraded the test to nothing more than a "recruiting guidance tool." The result is that a woman who doesn't meet the qualifications can still get a strenuous job. This is not the policy in Canada, where physical training standards in infantry boot camp were not lowered to accommodate women. In 1989, 101 out of 102 women failed to make the grade, so they didn't get the job.

Gender-norming, dual standards, flexible requirements, and "equivalent" training are counterproductive because they destroy the meaning of the word "qualified." In close combat all soldiers are interdependent; their lives depend on the strength, stamina, and speed of all unit members.

"Close combat" is defined as finding, closing with, and killing or capturing the enemy; it is more than the experience of being in danger. In that brutal environment, women don't have an equal opportunity to survive, or to help their fellow soldiers survive. It's not realistic to expect that for men war will be hell, but for women it will just be heck.

Congress Knows Best

Congress was pondering issues like this all summer, in response to an amendment sponsored by Representative Patricia Schroeder (D., Colo.) and approved by the House in May with little notice or public debate. The Schroeder amendment, and a companion measure sponsored by Edward Kennedy in the Senate, would begin the repeal of women's combat exemptions, starting with female aviators.

The Senate Armed Services Committee defeated Kennedy's amendment on an overwhelming bi-partisan vote. But the full Senate passed it in July, over the objections of the chiefs of the Army, Navy, Air Force, and Marines.

Together with other military witnesses, the service chiefs had testified that repeal of the law could not be limited to female aviators only. They warned that it would be impractical and politically untenable to bar women from Navy carriers on which fighter aircraft land. And because it would be inconsistent to treat enlisted women differently from officers, it would only be a matter of time before women were assigned—on the same *involuntary* basis as men—to all fighting units, including submarines, amphibious forces, tanks, and infantry.

There was strong but generally silent opposition from enlisted women, who will have to endure the worst of this—or give up their careers—if combat exemptions are repealed. Active-duty men and women who opposed the bill could not say so publicly without risking a negative mark in their personnel files. Aggressive female officers, on the other hand, swarmed door to door in the halls of Congress, taking advantage of the reluctance of Pentagon officials to enforce regulations against lobbying by uniformed personnel. The officer-lobbyists argued that combat exemptions are a barrier to career advancement, disregarding Defense Department figures that clearly indicate *all* military women are being consistently promoted at faster rates than men.

A conference committee will soon decide whether to rush ahead with repeal, or wait until a presidential commission determines what the financial costs and social consequences will be. In the meantime, accomplished, patriotic servicewomen who serve their country well may want to consider whether it is in their best interests for the Pentagon to continue taking direction from feminist activists with an ideological axe to grind.

The sexual incidents, for example, will never be ended as long as the military pretends that men and women are emotionless, perfectly interchangeable units whose physical differences can be disguised with unisex housing and gender-norming schemes.

Nor will family and child-care problems be resolved as long as the military promises more than it can possibly deliver. Before the next war begins, a balance must be found in the three-way conflict of interest among children, their parents, and the requirements of national defense.

The purpose of the military is not to provide jobs, promotions, and a laboratory for social experimentation; it is to deter aggression or win a war with as few casualties as possible. Nothing should be done that detracts from that responsibility.

EVE FATIGUE[3]

Eve Fatigue is an affliction that comes over a society that has had all the feminism it can stand. Say, for example, you are shopping by phone and the person taking your order for a shower curtain asks you what color you want.

"You have a choice—" You don't even hear the rest; your mind shuts down because every lurching move a woman makes is called a *choice*. The nullipara of all choices is, of course, abor-

[3]Article by Florence King, from *The National Review* N 18, 1991, 43:42. © 1991, *The National Review*, Inc. Reprinted with permission.

tion, but now feminists are saying that women should be able to *choose* whether to serve in combat, and rape victims should be allowed *choose* whether to let their names be published.

On June 18, during Senate Armed Services Committee hearings, the chiefs of the four military branches voiced such blunt objections to women in combat that they sounded Pattonesque. The Air Force representative frankly admitted that he considers male gender the premier qualification for a fighter pilot, and calmly justified his views with the first completely guiltless and public utterance to fall from the lips of a white male in two decades: "Maybe I'm wrong, but I can't help it, that's the way I feel."

Another sign that the Pentagon may be moving from the Potomac marshes to Eve Fatigue Flats was a July 1 news story about Captain Linda Bray, America's first war heroine, who liberated a dog kennel during the Panamanian action in 1989. Linda Bray is no longer in the army. She is now a housewife, her sporty look exchanged for frosted hair and long pointed nails painted "Maui Mango." As they say in Gothic novels, *What terrible thing happened to Linda Bray?*

She was hounded out of the Army.

Writes Scripps Howard reporter Peter Copeland: "When she and her company returned home to Fort Benning, Captain Bray was visited by investigators from the Army Criminal Investigation Division asking what had happened to the dogs at the kennel. A Panamanian soldier had accused American soldiers of killing the dogs several days after the invasion."

No one is more susceptible to Eve Fatigue than former feminist role models. Warning women against careers in the infantry the five-foot one, 105-pound Linda Bray recites a cautionary tale worthy of Phyllis Schlafly: "I carried too much weight. I always felt pressure in the military. 'You don't have very much weight in your rucksack. Why don't you carry a little more?' I kept adding more until my hips broke. I can't run, jump. I can't even go grocery shopping without having to sit down because it hurts."

Eve Fatigue replaced the seventh-inning stretch on July 5 when Washington's Orioles' baseball channel ran a Children's Defense Fund public-service ad. It shows a crowd of concerned citizens picketing a white marble government building. Some of the picketers are male, but the camera lingers on careerish women in business suits. One such woman has brought her baby in a carriage, but she gets so immersed in clamoring and petitioning that she leaves the carriage perched precariously at the top of a long marble staircase.

As the voice-over recites statistics on America's soaring rates of infant mortality, malnutrition, and child neglect and abuse, the baby carriage starts to roll backward down the steps. The statistics fly faster and faster, and so does the carriage. Finally the politically active mother remembers her child and turns around, but it's too late. As she watches in helpless horror, the bough breaks and down goes baby, cradle, and all.

Running this ad during a baseball game, when the viewership is overwhelmingly male, meets the definition of that ubiquitous act of our times known as "sending a message." Eve Fatigue is "on the table," and feminists are so panicked that *Washington Post* columnist Judy Mann detects that old devil "linkage" between a Betty Friedan speech and another news event of the same day.

"Ten minutes after she finished speaking," President Bush nominated Clarence Thomas to the Supreme Court. Four times, the President referred to him as 'the best man' for the job, suggesting that only men were considered. It was one of many ominous signs of what's to come."

Paranoia doesn't get any better than this.

PAT SCHROEDER: FIGHTING FOR MILITARY MOMS[4]

After almost 20 years in Congress, Pat Schroeder has learned she can't please all her supporters all of the time, but she is dismayed that her championing of women in the armed services causes such controversy. "I really get an awful lot of flak from women who normally support me saying they don't approve of my support for women in the military." Some feminists who admire Schroeder's constant critique of military waste and mismanagement find it incongruous for her to go to the barricades for women who are part of the war machine. "I keep saying feminism isn't about opening up the jobs you want, it's about opening up jobs some women may want. If I just opened up the jobs I wanted,

[4]Article by Anne Summers from *Ms.* My/Je 1991, 1:90–1. © 1991, *Ms.*. Reprinted with permission.

I wouldn't have to work so hard," retorts the most senior woman in Congress.

The military, says Schroeder, is "the last tree house," where women who want education and training are subjected to hostility, sexual harassment, and congressionally sanctioned obstacles to career development.

"I've always felt the women in the military got a really bum deal," she says. In addition to receiving feminist criticism, she says, "they get attacked by the Phyllis Schlaflys of the world and the guys in the military who don't want them. No one pats them on the head and says, 'Good job!' Instead they say, 'Should you really be here? Don't you feel bad that you're not home with your family?'"

Women soldiers shipping off to war became a familiar media theme of Operation Desert Storm, and it was reported that, given the choice, many women volunteered to go, even if this meant leaving young children behind. A new image, the military mom, was suddenly thrust into U.S. conciousness. With it came another kind of storm—over whether mothers should be sent into war zones where they risked capture or death. Once again, Pat Schroeder found herself in a minority position.

The military has to reduce its numbers of active-duty staff by 25 percent over the next few years, and Schroeder fears the public outcry about military mothers is simply playing into the Defense Department's hands. "You can imagine who they'd love to throw out first!" she said in a recent interview. "It doesn't make any difference how well they perform. Having people on the outside raising all these questions is really helpful to them [the DOD] because it gives them license to say, 'Well, gee, it's been really nice having you here. Now go home.'"

Schroeder opposes the bill of her feminist colleague, Congresswoman Barbara Boxer; the Military Orphans Prevention Act, currently before a House Armed Services subcommittee, would give the Defense Department discretion to exempt one parent at the request of a military couple—from serving in a combat zone. Such a policy could limit the advancement of parents, because, as Shirley Sagawa and Nancy Duff Campbell of the National Women's Law Center point out, "decisions regarding enlistment, training, and promotions rest on the individual's ability to perform during wartime."

Schroeder is angry with the Washington *Post*'s Sally Quinn—who wrote that sending mothers to war was an example of "feminism gone awry"—and other women who reject the "mommy track" in law firms but advocate it for the armed services. "If the *Post* had sent her to cover the war, she would have tried to get a Pulitzer prize and would have had a fit if someone said, 'You should stay home, you have small children.'"

The furor about mothers in the Gulf has raged out of proportion to the numbers involved. According to the Pentagon, the war left 17,500 families without the custodial parent. Of these about 1,200 were families with both parents in the Gulf. Of the rest, the great majority were families headed by single male. Schroeder favors family medical leave for military parents, as well as civilian parents—"the idea of taking mothers away from two-week-old babies is nonsense"—and wants the navy's four-month leave for new parents extended to all services.

When the first news stories appeared about men caring for their families while their wives went to war, Schroeder was elated. "My original hope was Wow! When this is over we're going to have a whole new group of people screaming for better child care, for family medical leave, all the stuff we've been trying to get in this country. But then it started to turn. We got this surly thing about America's going to feel much worse if a woman's a POW than if it's a man, and America should never send mothers; it's okay to send fathers."

Despite the debate, public support for women's participation in combat is surprisingly strong, according to CBS polls. Last October, 52 percent of those polled agreed women in Saudi Arabia should be in the fighting. This declined to 47 percent once the war actually began—but it was still a plurality over the 41 percent who opposcd women's combat involvement.

Early last year [1990], Schroeder introduced legislation to establish a four-year test for women to be deployed in combat units, something prevented by law in the navy and air force. The army simply refuses to assign women to such units. She couldn't get the support of even her Democratic colleagues. "They're so afraid of the 30-second ads that say, 'Your member of Congress voted to put your mother in combat boots,'" she says sadly.

Schroeder sees the combat restriction as just another job hurdle: "I say the only thing they protect women from is promotion. This war shows that I was right. They're indeed in the line of fire just like men are, and every bit as exposed to danger and attack." She likes to point out that modern combat doctrine requires that command headquarters and supply functions be targeted first, and it is precisely in these positions—away from the front line—that women are concentrated.

Schroeder's House Armed Services Committee will hold hearings with women who served in the Gulf and seek their views on how to deal with family separation, among other issues. Schroeder was aghast to learn that women had been sent to Saudi Arabia with "sanitation packages that had been put together in the forties," and that it took real effort for women to be issued tampons. "What I really want to hear is how they lived in those conditions day after day, how they lived in that basically apartheid-type world—it had to be awfully hard."

FEMINISM AND WAR[5]

A few military men may balk, but sending women into combat seems to be an idea whose time has come. It has become positively "illiberal" to resist the notion, for whatever the reason. In tune with America's at least temporarily impoverished political discourse, the issue is cast as one of "women's rights." Period.

One enthusiast for the "feminization" of combat is Representative Beverly Byron, Democrat of Maryland, chairwoman of the House Armed Services Subcommittee on Military Personnel and Compensation. Byron is cosponsoring a measure to repeal laws that bar women from flying combat planes. Talking about the idea, she could scarcely conceal her glee: "The argument that the country was not ready for women to be taken prisoners or come home in body bags is no longer an issue."

This seems an odd victory for women. But Representative Pat Schroeder, Democrat of Colorado, reassures us that a victory it is—a virtual revolution, in fact. She writes of the "historic

[5]Article by Jean Bethke Elshtain, Centennial Professor of Political Science and professor of Philosophy at Vanderbilt University, she is also author of *Women and War*. From *The Progressive*, S 1991, 55:14-16. © 1991, *The Progressive*. Reprinted with permission.

turnabout" on this issue and berates all who succumb to various myths—that women are weaker, need protecting, are physically incapable of handling combat, and so on. Not so, argues Schroeder: Anything you can do I can do better, or at least as well as. Women, she insists, are and must remain an "integral part of the U.S. armed forces," and current restrictions on our participation in combat are about one thing and one thing only—equal opportunity, keeping women "from promotions and career progression."

Carolyn Becraft, director of a project on the military for Women's Equity League, takes the same line, proclaiming: "This whole issue is about power, and whether women will be allowed to displace men in high-ranking positions." A pediatrician and feminist, Gwen Wurm of the University of Miami School of Medicine, weighs in with these words: "Nothing should be denied just because a woman has a uterus."

Equal opportunity. Rights. Power. Why am I dubious of the rhetoric of personal entitlement and advancement in the face of mothers separated from six-week-old babies, women in body bags, women POWs and a burnishing of the glamour of military life, now as women's work? My reservations are not about female ability in combat, but about what gets glossed over when we talk about the "glass ceiling" to women's "advancement" in the military.

The limited political and ethical vocabulary that seems to define the feminist position on this matter is especially troubling given women's historic involvement in the struggle for peace. I have no doubt that women can make war as well as men and that there are many women eager to do so.

Such women seized their opportunity to go to the Persian Gulf, including Second Lieutenant Anne Esposito, twenty-four, of the Eighty-second Airborne Division. "I wanted to do something high speed, low drag," she told a reporter. Roughly translated, this means "exciting, potentially dangerous." Staff Sergeant Liane Overstreet, thirty-four, with the 937th Engineer Group, proclaimed, "We're going to make history in this war. And I wouldn't have it any other way." There were others, though—particularly those forced to leave behond young children—who agonized over the Government's decision to send them to war. Their experience brings out the thorny problems involved in sending women into combat.

Let me lay my cards on the table. Unlike many others who write for *The Progressive*, I am not a pacifist. I do think that some war's have been necessary, albeit tragic and horrendous, as every war is and must be. I can envisage the possibility of wars that are just or that are fought in the interests of justice. So I am not per se anti-soldier. But I am concerned about our current national giddiness in the matter of war—specifically, about what gets hidden behind the much-trumpeted locution, "our men and women in the Gulf."

Women are 6 per cent of the overall force in Operation Desert Storm, some 32,350 of a total force of about 540,000. The staccato repetition of references to "our men and women" tended to disguise the lopsidedness of the rotation. Women are about 11 percent of our All Volunteer Force, so the numbers deployed were about one-half the proportion of women in the armed forces. Depending upon how one counts war and war-related deaths, the number of female casualties was between five and ten. Women served as supply pilots, mechanics, police officers, ordnance workers (putting bomb payloads into planes), and the usual array of clerical, nursing, and support services. Women did not serve and cannot serve in ground combat or on warships. But both houses of Congress have passed bills clearing the way for women to fly combat missions. And, as before, every other "job description" in the military is up for grabs.

This war not only put women in uniform closer to combat than ever before in our history, it marks a definitive signal that the United States is more willing to put more women offically in war danger zones than is any other country. Israel, for example, often invoked as a country with "women soldiers," exempts all married women from the military and reserves, and women in the Israel Defense Forces have no combat duties on land or sea. Opposition in Israel to placing women near the front lines is strong. During the 1980s in West Germany, when the possibility of requiring that women serve in the Bundeswehr came up in parliament, opposition was unrelenting, much of it coming from feminist groups. Soviet women formed the only regular female combat forces during World War II, but since then the Soviets have designated women as noncombatants and their huge army of 4.4 million includes only 10,000 women in clerical and medical positions.

The United States is on the front lines pushing back the definition of what is considered "equal opportunity." A good many women in the Army and civilians, male and female, appear to support this move, even as polling data indicate that differences between men and women on the wisdom of resorting to military force also continue to hold.

On the day the Gulf war started, a *USA Today* poll showed that 83 per cent of men and 67 per cent of women supported the effort. These differences, which narrowed as the war continued, are nevertheless remarkably consistent. Interestingly, slightly *more* women than men favored sending women on combat missions (74 to 71 percent), according to an NBC/*Wall Street Journal* poll completed six months before the Gulf war. If you add the findings of an Associated Press poll conducted during the war, in which 64 per cent of Americans overall rejected sending mothers of young children into the war zone, you get a picture of a society at odds with itself.

Military women, too, are divided. Those women with career aspirations in the military are gung-ho to waive combat exclusion clauses. But other women, primarily noncareerists in the reserves, harbor doubts. Those most in favor of placing women in combat are those most likely to benefit directly from earning their stripes in combat, and they are women most often quoted and celebrated in war and postwar media hyperventilation. CONQUERING HEROINES, hail slick magazines whose primary "target" is the "young adult." Sandwiched between paeans to eternal youth, smashing new styles, summer make-up and the like, one finds photographs of women, posed smartly, weapons at the ready. One article suggests that, in addition to doing their own jobs, women were also useful in the war effort because they provided a "shoulder to cry on" for the men. Military women described their contributions as "nurturing."

Life magazine detailed the 200-YEAR WAR TO LIBERATE THE MILITARY featuring a smug article entitled WOMEN'S WORK. The author, Jeannie Ralston, set out to destroy one "myth" after another, arguing that women proved definitely that they, too, could respond to the slogan BE ALL THAT YOU CAN BE. The most pernicious myth of all is "Mothers shouldn't—and don't want to—go to war." Sexist drivel, barks Ralston, we're in the era of role reversal and only whimps whine about mothers of children going to a war zone. Besides, "mothers had a positive effect in the Gulf"—the nurturing factor again, apparently—but despite this beneficial contribution politicans started to sponsor bills "excusing mothers from deployment."

The primary sponsor of such legislation was not a moss-gathering patriarch but liberal Representative Barbara Boxer, Democrat of California. Despite her pro-combat stance, Schroeder, too, indicated something should be done to prevent terrible hardship to children when their only parent (usually the mother) or both father and mother are deployed. The *Life* publicist for women in the military focused exclusively on the question of equal opportunity, and argued that 1) women sign a contract when they join the All Volunteer Force, and 2) the Army requires that parents have a "plan" for child care. So what's the problem?

The problem is not only that mothers of young children and the children themselves suffered from serious stress and trauma at separation—remember Specialist Fourth Class Hollie Vance bidding her seven-week-old daughter goodbye?—but what our inability to think about the children says about American society overall. Vance told a reporter she had never anticipated combat, "let alone right after I had my first child. I've built an ice wall around my heart to try and cool the pain." Surely this doesn't sound like a feminist victory to any but the most determined ideologue. The Persian Gulf war left children from 17,500 families "without the custodial single parent who usually cares for them or without both parents, according to Defense Department figures," *The Washington Post* reported.

Some 16,300 single parents were deployed, as were 1,200 military couples with children. A number of mothers, who had never dreamed they would be kept in anything other than a stateside backup capacity, balked at going. One mother of a twenty-one-month-old child and a five-month-old nursing baby was called up and said she had been misled by the Air Force. She pleaded to be able to wean her baby, "but they said no. . . . It's a nightmare." Another mother, Faith Stewart, got her orders and went into labor the next day. "It's outrageous to separate a mother and her new baby," she said. "I think it's totally wrong sending both parents over there."

The Army claimed it hadn't foreseen the "Gulf orphan" problem (the Army was at the forefront of this issue, having far more women than any other branch). It couldn't, it claimed, predict the reports of kids blaming themselves for their parents' absence, and becoming disruptive, sleepless, aggressive, and jittery; of children traumatized by being uprooted from their neighborhoods and communities after having been severed from their mothers and fathers. Belatedly, Representative Boxer tried to address this situation when she introduced legislation in the House to prevent both of a child's parents from being sent to a war zone.

Of course, no one with what my mother calls "the good sense of a goose" thinks it is a good thing for infants to be yanked away from nursing mothers. Surely we don't need experts to tell us that. But, then, perhaps we do if we keep hearing the riposte, this from Becky Constantino, chairwomen of the Defense Advisory Committee on Women in the Services, who opined that the "Gulf Orphan's Bill" signaled nothing less than a setback for women's rights. "We've worked tirelessly to get equal opportunities for women to serve and we do not want those opportunities set back," she told *The Tennessean*, explaining her opposition to legal protection for "Gulf orphan" children.

To present this issue as one of pro- or anti-women's rights is to vulgarize. Rather, it is a matter of striking a balance, as Ellen Goodman put it. In one of the several stories of abandonment during wartime, Goodman, a women's rights advocate, cited Boxer with favor. "This is a voluntary army, but these aren't volunteer children," she wrote in the *Boston Globe*. The war-orphans bill, wrote Goodman, "takes the side, not of the parents or the Army, but of children." "Overlooking the fact that only women become pregnant and nurse babies requires a great leap of the imagination, but once the Pentagon gets an idea in its head, it is hard to stop it," wrote columnist Mary McGrory. The Pentagon, she said, "has formalized indefensible indifference toward children." Not just the Pentagon, but that brand of feminism best tagged rights absolutism.

If anything, the experiences of many of the mothers who went to the Gulf point up the need for a different kind of leadership from women—not only to pave the way for women's individual advancement through the ranks, but to lead us to a better balance in our country's priorities. A society that puts its children dead last is a society progressing rapidly toward moral ruin. If women do not turn their attention toward fighting this destructive momentum, who will?

THE FEMINIST ASSAULT ON THE MILITARY[6]

For nearly two decades after the Sixties, the military remained the one institution to withstand the baleful influences of the radical Left. Now that the cold war is over, this immunity appears to have ended. A series of relatively trivial incidents (a joke about women's sexual excuses, a skit mocking a female member of Congress) and a drunken party at which crotches were grabbed in a gantlet ritual have fueled a national hysteria about "sexual harassment" and a political witchhunt that is threatening to deconstruct the military in the way other institutions have been deconstructed before.

Fanning the fires are feminist legislators on the Armed Services Committee, led by Democrat Pat Schroeder, who want women assigned to combat roles. In a July 9 letter to Defense Secretary Dick Cheney, Representative Schroeder put the Pentagon on notice that Tailhook was only "a symptom" and that the resignation of Navy Secretary Garrett does not begin "to address the problem." Mrs. Schroeder called for investigations and prosecutions to purge the Navy of sexual miscreants and bad attitudes.

Mrs. Schroeder herself was the center of the second Navy "scandal," over the Tom Cat Follies at the Miramar Naval Station. The Follies, which were held in a private officers' club and which traditionally include off-color jibes at Navy brass, featured lampoons of George Bush and Dan Quayle. But it was the two skits about Representative Schroeder that caused heads to roll. The first was an altered nursery rhyme: "Hickory, dickory dock, Pat Schroeder s—-ed my c—-" The second was a skit in which Mrs. Schroeder went to Europe for a sex-change operation and came back incarnated as Dick Cheney. Not far off the mark, considering that Mrs. Schroeder has been mentioned as a possible Secretary of Defense in a Clinton Administration and that Mr. Cheney has been timid on the issue of women in combat.

When the Navy brass was alerted to the contents of the show by a female officer who had been present, the reaction was swift. Five career officers present at the Follies had their commands ter-

[6]Article by David Horowitz from *The National Review*, 44:46-9, O 5 '92. ©1992, *The National Review*, Inc. Reprinted by permission.

minated. (Subsequently, two were reinstated.) The Navy has also apologized to Mrs. Schroeder. Such appeasement, however, has only whetted the appetite of the feminist vanguard, which has stepped up its campaign to pass the Schroeder Amendment, allowing women to fly combat missions. It is seen by advocates as a "wedge" measure that would lead to expanded combat roles and true "institutional equality" for women. A Presidential Commission appointed to review the issue is scheduled to make a recommendation in November.

Militantly Anti-Military

It should come as no surprise that many advocates of the change have previously shown little interest in maintaining an effective defense. Representative Schroeder, for example, was an antiwar activist before entering the House. She has been a determined adversary of military preparedness on the Armed Services Committee, where she now serves as a ranking member along with Beverly Byron (who has demanded that every officer merely *present* at Tailhook be thrown out of the service) and radical Congressman Ron Dellums, who denounced Jimmy Carter as "evil" for opposing Soviet aggression in Afghanistan.

When New Left radicals, like myself, launched the movement against the war in Vietnam, we did not say we wanted the Communists to win—which we did. We said we wanted to bring the troops home, which accomplished our objective: the Communists won. With disastrous consequences for Vietnam and the world.

Examples of this kind of double agenda abound in the current feminist campaign and can be found in testimony before the Presidential Commission on the Assignment of Women in the Armed Forces. Maria Lepowsky, a professor of Women's Studies, provided the commissioners with data to support a combat role for women. Then Professor Lepowsky asked herself: "What would be some possible consequences . . . —if women were put in combat—on American cultural values and American society . . . ?" She answered her own question: "I think there might be increased concern about committing troops to combat, also perhaps a good thing. . . . "

In other words, Professor Lepowsky was advocating that women be put in combat roles because to do so would make it *more difficult* to commit troops to combat. Now this is a kind of candor that is unusual for the Left.

Reform, Soviet Style

Moderate feminists generally want modest reforms in American society. Technological advances, like birth control, have dramatically changed women's social roles, requiring adjustments in the culture. The most constructive way for these changes to take place is deliberately, and with due respect for consequences that may be unforeseen. As the inhabitants of the former Soviet empire discovered, at great human cost, revolutionary cures can often be worse than the disease.

This is a lesson lost on feminism's radical wing. When advocates of current military reform speak of "gender integration" of the military, they are often invoking the ideas of these radicals without recognizing them for what they are. Gender feminism is a bastard child of Marxism. It holds that women are not women by nature, but that society has "constructed" or created them female so that men could oppress them. Gender feminists are social engineers in the same way as Communists. They deny that human biology fundamentally influences who we are. For them, the solution to all social problems, conflicts, and disappointments in life is to manipulate laws and institutions so as to create liberated human beings, who will not hate, have prejudices, exhibit bad sexual manners, or go to war.

Gender feminists have little interest in questions of America's national security because they believe America is a patriarchal, sexist, racist oppressor whose institutions must be transformed beyond recognition. Of course, the gender feminists are not so naïve as to admit their radical agendas outside the sanctuaries of women's studies departments. In testifying before Presidential Commissions they will say that placing women in combat positions is merely an extension of women working outside the home, and of equal opportunity.

But placing women in harm's way and training them to kill one-on-one is not a mere extension of working outside the home. Furthermore, there are definite limits to equal rights and equal opportunity when biology is involved. Do American males have the right to bear children? Do they have an equal opportunity with women to do so? Do they have an equal aptitude for combat? Ninety percent of those arrested for violent crimes are male. Obviously males have a distinct advantage over females in mobilizing an existing instinct for aggression for the purpose of organized combat.

The difficulty in confronting these issues on their merits is the emotional element that is introduced by the moral posturing of the Left. One of the leading advocates of equal military roles is Commander Rosemary Mariner, a 19-year career naval officer. Commander Mariner's testimony before the Commission is illustrative: "As with racial integration the biggest problem confronting gender integration is not men or women, but bigotry. It is bigotry that is the root cause of racial and sexual harassment. From common verbal abuse to the criminal acts of a Tailhook debacle, sexual harassment will continue to be a major problem in the armed forces because the combat exclusion law and policies make women institutionally inferior."

The basic elements of the radical view are all here. Sexual relations between men and women are encompassed by the paradigm of racial relations between black and whites. The problem of sexual harassment is unrelated to the different biologies and sexual drives of men and women. The real problem is an institutional framework that causes women to be perceived as inferior. In the eyes of the gender feminists, if women were included in combat (and thus treated as the equals they are), if gender roles were abolished, then sexual harassment would cease to be a "major problem."

Consider the proposition: For five thousand years men have been more aggressive sexually than women. In recognition of this, for five thousand years the sexual rules for men and women have been different. And for the same period, many men, failing to heed those rules, have overstepped the boundaries of decent behavior. But now we are to believe that is merely the past. According to the gender feminists, the U.S. military, by including women in combat positions, can solve this age-old problem. As soon as this law is changed, women's self-esteem will rise, men's respect for women will increase, and presto! sexual harassment will cease.

It is difficult to believe that a rational human being could propose such nonsense, but this is the fundamental idea that feminists advance *ad nauseam*, and that our military brass and political leadership are capitulating to at a disturbing pace.

This summer, Jerry Tuttle, a three-star admiral who had been nominated by the President for one of the top 12 posts in the Navy, saw his career run into a wall, as the President was forced to withdraw his nomination. Why? Because a newsletter for which he was responsible printed the following joke: *Beer is better than women because beer never has a headache.*

What is going on in America when a three-star admiral can lose a promotion over a lame joke that he didn't even make? How could a Republican President cave in to pressures like this, and why isn't there national outrage over it? And what is the problem with feminists who can't handle this kind of trivia? Yet they want to enter a war zone and engage in combat!

Studies conducted at West Point have identified 120 physical differences between men and women that bear on military requirements. Yet the U.S. Naval Academy has been criticized for not moving fast enough to increase its female enrollment. Senator Barbara Mikulski has demanded "an attitude change" at the academy, and an official Committee on Women's Issues headed by Rear Admiral Virgil Hill has called for the "immediate dismissal of senior officers who question the role of women in the military." To question—to *question*—the role of women in the military is now regarded as bigotry by the military itself.

The word "bigot" has resonance. It is meant to invoke the specter of racism and to appropriate the moral mantle of the civil-rights movement for feminist causes. This feminist attempt to hijack the civil-rights movement is both spurious and offensive, but it is highly effective in preventing opponents from laughing feminist arguments out of court.

As for the facts about women's suitability for combat, it is not always easy to discover them. In its Washington session in June, the Presidential Commission heard testimony from William S. Lind, former defense advisor to Gary Hart. Lind referred to the suppression of information vital to the decisions the Commission is being asked to make. According to Lind, the Army Personnel Office had detailed information on problems encountered with women troops in Desert Storm, which had not been released to the public. The information included the fact that, when the troops were called to battle, the non-deployability rate for women was three to four times higher than that for men. This had a negative effect on unit cohesion, a primary component of combat effectiveness. Pregnancy during Desert Shield was the primary reason for nondeployability.

Also covered up are the consequences of the way women are treated in the service academies. The official position at West Point, for example, is that there have been no negative effects.

The facts are different, as a recent Heritage study by Robert Knight reveals. According to the sworn testimony of a West Point official taken in a Roanoke court, when men and women are required to perform the same exercises, women's scores are "weighted" to compensate for their deficiencies; women cadets take "comparable" training when they cannot meet the physical standards for male cadets, and peer ratings have been eliminated because women were scoring too low. "Gender norming"—the institutionalization of a double standard, so that women are measured against other women, rather than against men—is now the rule at all the service academies.

Even the *men's* training program has been downgraded: cadets no longer train in combat boots because women were experiencing higher rates of injury; running with heavy weapons had been eliminated because it is "unrealistic and therefore inappropriate" to expect women to do it; the famed "recondo" endurance week, during which cadets used to march with full backpacks and undergo other strenuous activities, has been eliminated as have upper-body strength events in the obstacle course.

It is one thing to have second-rate professors because of affirmative-action quotas that lower standards. But second-rate officer corps?

Not surprisingly, resentment on the part of male cadets is high. One indication is that more than 50 per cent of the women cadets at West Point reported that they had been sexually harassed last year.

It is a perfectly sinister combination. Rub men's noses in arbitrariness and unfairness, and then charge them with sexual harassment when they react. It is also a perfect prescription for accumulating power and controlling resources. Which is what this witchhunt is ultimately about. For every male who falls from grace there is a politically correct career officer or politician ready to achieve grace by prosecuting the cause. Rosemary Mariner is a candidate for admiral; Beverly Byron has been mentioned for Secretary of the Navy; Pat Schroeder has her sights set on being Secretary of Defense.

Another problem raised by William Lind is what happens when women troops are actually deployed. In combat situations, men will act instinctively to protect women, abandoning their tactical objectives in the process. The males' protective instincts will be increased by the knowledge of what other males will do to females taken prisoner. This is not theory, but the experience of the Israelis and other military forces that tried and then abandoned the practice of deploying women in combat.

No amount of sensitivity training, no amount of brainwashing can alter human nature. The Communists proved this at unbelievable cost. They could not make a new socialist man (or woman) who would respond as effectively and efficiently to administrative commands as to market incentives, who would be communists and not individualist. The Communists killed tens of millions of people and impoverished whole nations trying to change human nature, all the time calling it "liberation," just as radical feminists do. It didn't work.

And yet, the military leadership presses on. The Air Force has established a SERE program (Survival, Evasion, Resistance, and Escape), including its own "prisoner of war" camp in Washington state to desensitize its male recruits so that they won't react like men when female prisoners are tortured. In their infinite wisdom, Mrs. Schroeder and her feminist colleagues have enlisted the military in a program to brainwash men so they won't care what happens to women. That's consciousness raising, feminist style.

It is hardly necessary to have the detailed information that the military has decided to suppress, to see that America's ability to wage war has always been seriously weakened by the deployment of relatively large numbers of women to an overseas battlefield, even absent a combat role. Who does not remember the poignant story the networks did, in lavish detail, about the children left behind by their mothers dispatched to war duty in the Persian Gulf? (In fact there were 16,337 single military parents who left anxious children behind.)

The net result is that an American President now is under pressure to win a war in four days or lose the war at home. What will be the temptation for dictators to test the will of America's liberated military and compassionate citizenry? These changes have implications for diplomacy and for long-term national-security interests that are literally incalculable.

The fabric of America's institutional and cultural life has already been shredded by the forces of the Left, with disastrous social consequences. Now the purpose and mission of the American military are held to be of less concern than the need to eradicate any possible injustice that might be associated with the exclusion of women from combat. The worst crimes of our century have been committed by crusades to eradicate injustice, stamp out politically incorrect attitudes, and reconstruct human nature. Let's not add the weakening of America's military to the depressing list of disasters of these utopias that failed.

THE NEW TOP GUNS[7]

During the Persian Gulf war, women distinguished themselves in the cockpits of helicopters, midair refueling tankers and the lumbering C-141 transport jets that ferried troops across enemy lines. Their performance and that of all the 35,000 women who served in the gulf has generated support in Congress and public opinion for broadening the role of females in the military. Last week in a landmark move the Senate voted overwhelmingly to overturn a 43-year-old law that bars women from flying combat missions. Said Delaware Senator William Roth, who cosponsored the amendment with Senator Edward Kennedy of Massachusetts: "The facts show that women pilots have successively broken ground in just about every area of aviation—and they deserve the opportunity to compete."

The new measure, which would allow but not require each of the services to certify women pilots for combat missions, won little support among the military brass. Said former Marine Commandant Robert H. Barrow: "Women give life. Sustain life. Nurture life. They don't take it." Despite such reservations, the Pentagon is, likely to go along grudgingly with the policy.

Opponents of the measure, including Sam Nunn, chairman of the Senate Armed Services Committee, had argued that a presidential study commission should precede any green light for women fighter pilots. Though they failed to preserve the aviation ban, adherents of this go-slow approach won support for a 15-member White House-named panel that would present a report to Congress next year [1992] on the feasibility of admitting women to a wide variety of combat jobs.

[7]Article by Julie Johnson, from *Time*, Ag 12, 1991, 138:31. © 1991, *Time, Inc.* Reprinted with permission.

Supporters of the new policy argue that combat missions are an essential stepping-stone to promotions. While, for example, women account for 9.9% of the enlisted personnel and lO.5% of the officers in the Air Force, they are virtually absent at the senior-officer level. Of the service's 333 generals, only three are women. "The opponents talk about sex and toilets, but this fight is really about privilege and power," says military analyst and former Army Captain Carolyn H. Becraft.

Women are not unanimous in supporting the idea of females in combat. Even within the armed forces, combat lust is more widspread among female officers than enlisted servicewomen. "What we're seeing," says Charles Moskos, a military sociologist at Northwestern University, "is a push by female officers and civilian feminists." Moskos and others argue that introducing the notion of combat equality may sharply reduce the number of women who enlist and could cause problems in the future if the draft is ever reinstated.

Fears that the limited measure adopted last week will lead to a battlefield role for women are probably exaggerated. "I really doubt that it will open the floodgates," says Martin Binkin, a Brookings Institution expert on women in combat. "I don't see a lot of women eager to go." But some women do want to do the job, and in an era in which the high-technology blurs battle lines and brains may edge out brawn, there is no good reason to deny them the chance.

SHOULD MOMS GO TO WAR?[8]

It was a sight we will never forget: children desperately clinging to their mothers before they were shipped off to war. No one who saw that painful emotional exchange between the first women deployed to the Persian Gulf and their children could remain unaffected. And many questioned whether mothers should be leaving their families for war at all.

[8]Article by Richette L. Haywood, from *Jet*, Mr 4, 1991. © 1991, Johnson Publishing Company, Inc. Reprinted with permission.

Even now, several weeks into the war, the memory still pulls on the heartstrings of all Americans, and the reality of mothers fighting in the Persian Gulf is striking strong and divisive chords across the nation.

"There are instances of babies as young as two-weeks-old being separated from their mothers . . . ," said Rep. Patricia Schroeder (D., Colo.), a senior member of both the House Armed Services Committee and the Select Committee on Children, Youth and Families. This is the predicament that has Americans questioning whether we are winning the war, but losing the family.

With approximately 6 percent or 31,000 of the 513,000 United States all-volunteer military personnel deployed to Desert Storm being female, the roles of women, particularly mothers, has politicians and the public trying to work through the obvious risks. The broad range of questions and concerns associated with this country's largest wartime call-up of women fluctuate from fairness to foolishness.

"You can't imagine my feeling," says T.M. Harris, who suddenly found herself the principal caretaker of her three grandchildren when her single-parent 42-year-old daughter, Army Reserve Sgt. Sharon Harris, was unexpectedly deployed to Desert Storm on Valentine's Day before being able to make other arrangements. "I am a sick 70-year-old woman with three children," explains Harris, a native of Jamaica who flew from her home in Canada to Brooklyn, N.Y., to become guardian of her granddaughters Leanika, 2½, Kimberlea, 13, and Janice, 18.

Although she knows precious little about the day-to-day intricacies of the United States business structure—such as the banking system, mass transportation, etc.—combined with the fact that she suffers from numerous physical ailments which limit her mobility and ability to care for the children, Harris' resolve to make the trip was solely of a maternal nature. It was family calling.

"I had to come to protect the children," she says with a ring of desperation in her voice as her toddler granddaughter's voice can be heard in the background making a symphony of appeals for grandmother's undivided attention.

"I think its an atrocity," said Karen Daughtry, chief organizer of Mothers Against War. Wife of Brooklyn's House of the Lord Pentecostal Churches pastor Rev. Herbert Daughtry, Mrs.

Daughtry, who has four adult children of her own, was moved to establish the organization during a church vigil the night bombing began in Kuwait. She declares, "I know of some instances personally of women being called up and having to leave their children. . . . A good friend's daughter has been called-up and she was just two credits away from earing a master's degree. Now she's in Saudi Arabia. And many of our (Black) women went in (the military) because they didn't have any other way to get an education."

Irrespective of individual reasons for joining the military, the reality is plain: they *volunteered* to be a cog in Uncle Sam's fighting machine. As such, the responsibilities and risks for volunteers has always been crystal clear.

"I have no problem with women going over there. They knew what the possibilities were when they joined. They can do the job," says James Mosby, of Petersburg, Va., whose Army Reservist wife, Aheila, was called to Saudi Arabia in mid-February. "Sheila has been in the reserves a long time (since 1979), and its just unfortunate that all of this happened at once," relates Mosby, himself a former serviceman. Because of the speed in which his wife was deployed confided Mosby, he was denied the opportunity of even a goodbye kiss from the mother of his 9-month-old daughter, Kayla, at a time when "now I kind of have to be father and mother."

The stories of hindrances and hardships faced by families of mothers at war seem crushing, if not endless. According to the U.S. Defense Department at JET press time, while there were no gender breakdowns on the number, there were approximately 16,300 single-parents participating in Desert Storm and approximately 1,200 dual-military couples.

"The policy," explained Maj. Doug Hart, of the Defense Department, "is that all members of the military can be deployed worldwide. . . . Women, 42-days after (giving) birth, if there are no medical problems, are able to be deployed." Within the individual branches of the military, pointed out Hart, the policy "is very, very lenient," even allowing parents making appeals of hardship to be discharged or stationed where they can care for their children. But while there is some license for individual interpretation, the military's policy is indisputable: Mothers, who for so long were banned from military service, should not be easily let out of their commitments.

Sen. John Heinz (R., Pa.), has introduced a bill exempting single parents and one parent of a military couple from combat duty or being in an "imminent danger" zone. A similar bill in the House would allow the Pentagon to determine which parent would be exempted.

Additionally, Rep. Schroeder, in a recent letter, appealed to Secretary of Defense Dick Cheney "to immediately institute a service-wide parental leave policy allowing servicemembers who are mothers ans fathers of newborn or newly adopted children up to 18 weeks of parental leave . . . Child development experts are unanimous in concluding that the most critical stages of the parent-child relationship takes place within the first four months of the baby's life."

Pediatrician Dr. Joyce L. Whitaker, who is in private practice and on staff at four hospitals in Richmond, Va., explains that "unlike a typical separation, when a parent goes to work, this is different because it carries the connotation that the parent may not come back." But even if the mother returns, a long-term separation from her child could compromise the relationship, she summarizes. "The closest person to a child has been pulled away," says Whitaker, "And that could be detrimental. An infant might even forget his mother."

Mothers Against War organizer, Daughtry agrees. She maintains that "the military needs to sort out and sort through who can best leave to serve the country without doing havoc to the families back here." In the midst of the debate are innocent and confused children.

"The children don't really understand how far away the war is," contends Walker Mill Middle School Principal Joan Brown, who has a number of students who are children of parents stationed at Andrews Air Force Base, outside of Washington, D.C., enrolled at her Prince Georges County, Md., school. "They think they are in imminent danger here. They are frightened when they see the gas masks. Children from Andrews Air Force Base are particularly concerned when they see signs every time they enter the post about possible terrorists attacks."

[One example] . . . of the way youngsters are viewing the war, says Brown, who has instituted an open-door counseling policy for children experiencing anxiety about the war, occurred recently during lunch when a student stopped "me to ask if I was saved."

Youngsters are fearing the worse, say child advocacy groups. Children's Defense Fund President Marian Wright Edelman, whose organization supports exempting one parent from combat duty, told an interviewer children fear "that they will be abandoned forever by both parents. . . . We obviously have to balance the needs of children and the responsibility of parents with the needs of the war." She further contends, "War is an extremely stressful event for children. We just need to think about the impact on them."

The impact on military personnel's children will depend on their relationship with their parent prior to the war, asserts Christella Cain, a counselor at Bowie High School in Austin, Tx., who is advising students with parents serving in the Gulf and is also licensed by the state as a professional counselor.

"When the child is living day-in-and-day-out with the mother, it is a heavy blow on the child to be separated," Cain contends, pointing to the fact that in the American family structure "generally mother's do most of the nurturing. And most children miss that more than anything else." Fortunately, she adds, the bonding between mother and child "can most certainly be resumed when she returns."

However, "something is going to be missing, particularly with infants and younger children because the mother missed being there during the time when the child was first beginning to interact with (whom ever was serving) as the mother figure," says Whitaker.

REQUIEM FOR A SOLDIER[9]

The American Flag was draped over the gunmetal-gray coffin at a funeral home in Oradell, N.J. On a table to the left of the coffin was an 8-by-10 photo of a smiling, somewhat shy-looking woman wearing a soft pastel suit and pearls. On the right was quite another photograph, of a leaner-faced woman with a cocky

[9]Article by Linda Bird Francke, from *The New York Times Magazine*, Ap 21, 1991, p. 24–25.

grin, hands on the hips of her desert camouflage uniform, an Army helicopter of the Second Batttalion, 159th Aviation immediately behind her.

I drove three hours to Maj. Marie T. Rossi's wake and returned the next day for her funeral. I'd never met the chopper pilot whose helicopter had hit a microwave tower near a Saudi pipeline, the commanding officer of Company B who'd clung to civilized living in the desert by laying a "parquet" floor of half-filled sandbags in her tent, the woman who, after Sunday services, invited the chaplain back to share the Earl Grey tea her mother had sent her.

I was planning to interview Major Rossi when she returned to the States, to try to understand why she and so many other bright and thoughtful women were choosing careers in the military. Like many other civilians, I had been stunned to learn the numbers of women serving in the armed forces. If there hadn't been a war, I never would have known. Because there'd been a war, I'd now never know Major Rossi.

Watching the war on television, I'd vacillated between feelings of awe and uneasiness at women in their modern military roles. It was jolting to see young women loading missiles on planes and aching to fly fighter jets in combat. On the other hand, I admired these military women for driving six-wheel trucks and shinnying in and out of jet engine pods. A final barrier seemed to be breaking down between the sexes. But at what cost? Looking at the military funeral detachment as it wheeled Major Rossi's coffin into St. Joseph's Church, I tried to summon up pride for a fallen soldier, but instead felt sadness for a fallen sister.

As Major Rossi's friends and relatives spoke, I recalled an August evening soon after the Iraqi invasion of Kuwait when my daughters were home on vacation and several of their male friends dropped by. The young men, juniors and seniors in college, were pale and strained, talking anxiously about the possibility of a military draft. My daughters, 19 and 21 years old, were chattering on about their hopes for interesting jobs after graduation. It hadn't seemed fair. Here were my girls—healthy, strong graduates of Outward Bound, their faces still flushed from a pre-dinner run—talking freely about the future. And here were the boys whose futures suddenly seemed threatened.

I didn't know what to think. I still don't. As a feminist and my own sort of patriot, I feel that women and men should share equally in the burdens and the opportunities of citizenship. But the new military seems to have stretched equality to the breaking point. The surreal live television hookup between a family in the States and a mother in the desert reminding them where the Christmas ornaments were stored smacked of values gone entirely awry. Yet this woman, like the 29,000 others in the gulf, had voluntarily signed on to serve. What siren song had the military sung to them?

To ground myself in this growing phenomenon, I'd taken my younger daughter to a recruiting station in Riverhead, L.I. Each branch of the military had an office—the Army, the Navy, the Air Force, the Marines. The recruiters were very persuasive. "When you graduate, do you think any employer is going to be banging on your door in this economy?" the Marine recruiter asked her. "Think about it. You're out of college. Your Mom breaks your plate. Your Dad turns your bedroom into a den. You're on your own. Now what do you do?" He gave me a decal: "My daughter is a United States Marine."

The Air Force recruiter was easier to resist. "Have you ever had problems with the law?" he grilled my daughter. "Have you ever been arrested, ever gotten a traffic ticket? Have you ever sold, bought, trafficked, brought drugs into the country, used drugs?" Instead of a decal, he gave us a copy of "High Flight," the romantic World War II poem President Reagan had used to eulogize the crew of the Challenger. "Oh, I have slipped the surly bonds of earth and danced the skies on laughter-silvered wings" it begins. The Air Force recruiter did not mention the fact that the poem's author, John Gillespie Magee Jr., had died in the war at the age of 19.

There is no talk of death in recruiting offices, no talk of danger or war or separation from families. The operative words are "opportunity," "education," "technical skills" and "training." The Marine recruiter added another military carrot by pulling out a sheet of paper with newspaper want ads Scotch-taped to it. "Every job opening requires skills. But how do you get them? We give them to you." My daughter's face began to flush. "If we don't get out of here in 30 seconds, I'm going to sign up," she muttered.

Those in the military know about death, of course. They get on-the-job training. Major Rossi's husband, Chief Warrant Officer John Anderson Cayton, told the mourners at her funeral that he had prayed hard for his wife's safety while he was serving in

Kuwait. His were not prayers that come on Hallmark cards. "I prayed that guidance be given to her so that she could command the company, so she could lead her troops in battle," said the tall young man in the same dress blue Army uniform he'd worn to their wedding just nine months before. "And I prayed to the Lord to take care of my sweet little wife."

Habits fade away slowly, just like old soldiers. When I called Arlington National Cemetery to confirm the time of Major Rossi's burial, I was told "he" was down for 3 P.M. on March 11.

"She," I corrected the scheduler gently.

"His family and friends will gather at the new administration building," the scheduler continued.

"*Her* family and friends," I said more firmly. "Major Rossi is a woman."

"Be here at least 15 minutes early," she said. "We have a lot of burials on Monday."

Hundreds of military women turned out at Arlington, wearing stripes and ribbons and badges indecipherable to most civilians. I caught a ride with three members of the Women Auxiliary Service Pilots, the Wasps, who flew during World War II. One was wearing her husband's shirt under her old uniform. The shirts sold at the PX with narrow enough shoulders, she explained, don't fit over the bust.

No one knows how many women are buried in their own military right under the 220,000 pristine headstones at Arlington. The cemetery's records do not differentiate between genders or among races and religions.

"If the women were married, you could walk around and count the headstones that say 'Her husband,' rather than 'His wife,'" suggested an Arlington historian. "I've seen a few and always noticed them." Arlington is going to run out of room by the year 2035; a columbarium will provide 100,000 niches for the ashes of 21st century soldiers. How many of them will be women?

The military pageant of death, no doubt, will remain the same. Six black horses pulled the caisson carrying Major Rossi's coffin. Seven riflemen fired the 21-gun salute, the band softly played "America the Beautiful" and a solitary bugler under the trees blew taps. Major Rossi's husband threw the first spadeful of dirt on his wife's coffin, her brother, the second. It was a scene we're going to have get used to in the new military of ours, as we bury our sisters, our mothers, our wives, our daughters.

BIBLIOGRAPHY

An asterisk (*) preceding a reference indicates an excerpt from the work has been reprinted in this compilation.

Books and Pamphlets

Barkalow, Carol and Raab, Andrea. In the men's house; an inside account of life in the Army by one of West Point's first female graduates. Poseidon Press. '90.

Binkin, Martin & Bach, Shirley J. Women and the military. Brookings Institution. '77.

Blanco, Richard L. The war of the American Revolution; a selected annotated bibliography of published sources. Garland. '84.

Campbell, D' Ann. Women at war with America; private lives in a patriotic era. Harvard Univ. Press. '84.

Center of Military History/ Staff Support Branch. Women in combat and as military leaders. '80.

Claghorn, Charles Eugene. Women patriots of the American Revolution; a biographical dictionary. Scarecrow Press. '91.

Cooper, Helen. Arms and the woman. Univ. of North Carolina Press. '89.

Cornum, Rhonda, with Peter Copeland. She went to war; the Rhonda Cornum story. Presidio. '92.

Dorn, Edwin & Aspin, Les. Who defends America? Joint Center for Political Studies Press. '89.

Earley, Charity Adams. One woman's army; a black officer remembers the WAC. Texas A&M Univ. Press. '89.

Elshtain, Jean Bethke and Tobias, Sheila. Women, militarism, and war. Rowman & Littlefield. '90.

Enloe, Cynthia H. Does khaki become you?; the militarisation of women's lives. Pluto Press. '83. South End Press. '83.

Gibish, Jane E. Women in the armed forces. Air Univ. Library. '86.

Goldman, Nancy L. Female soldiers—combatants or noncombatants?; historical and contemporary perspectives. Greenwood Press. '82.

Harrell, Karen Fair. Women in the armed forces: a bibliography, 1970–1980. Vance Bibliographies. '80.

Hartmann, Susan M. The home front and beyond; American women in the 1940s. Harvard Univ. Press. '82.

Higonnet, Margaret R., ed. Behind the lines; gender and the two world wars. Yale Univ. Press, '87.

*Holm, Jeanne. Women in the military; an unfinished revolution. Presidio. '92.

Hosek, James R. and Peterson, Christine E. United States/ Office of the Assistant Secretary of Defense/Force Management and and Personnel. Serving Her Country. Rand Corp. '90.

Keil, Sally Van Wagenen. Those wonderful women in their flying machines. Rawson, Wade. '79.

MacCloskey, Monro. Your future as a woman in the armed forces. Rosen. '79.

Marshall, Kathryn. In the combat zone. Penguin. '88; Little Brown. '87.

Marshall, Catherine, Ogden, C.K. and Florence, Mary Sargant. Militarism versus feminism. Virago Press, 1987.

Marwick, Arthur. Women at war, 1914–1918. Croom Helm. '77.

Mitchell, Brian. Weak link; the feminization of the american military. Regnery Gateway. '89.

Noggle, Anne. For God, country, and the thrill of it. Texas A&M Univ. Press. '90.

Prior, Billy. Flight to glory. Ponce Press. '85.

Rogan, Helen. Mixed company. Beacon Press. '82. Putnam. '81.

Rothblum, Esther D. and Cole, Ellen, eds. One woman's recovery from the trauma of war. Hawthorne Press. '86.

Rustad, Michael. Women in khaki; the American enlisted women. Praeger. '82.

Salmonson, Jessica Amanda. The encyclopedia of Amazons; women warriors from antiquity to the modern era. Paragon. '91.

Saywell, Shelley. Women in war. Viking. '85.

Scharr, Adela Riek. Sisters in the sky. Patrice Press. '86.

Seeley, Charlotte Palmer and Purdy, Virginia Cardwell. American women and the U.S. armed forces. National Records and Archives. '92.

Segal, David R. and Sinaiko, H. Wallace. Life in the rank and file. Pergamon-Brassey's Int. Defense. '86.

Schneider, Dorothy and Schneider, Carl J. Sound off!; American military women speak out. Dutton. '88. Paragon. '92.

——. Into the breach; American women overseas in World War I. Viking. '91.

Slappey, Mary McGowan. Exploring military service for women. Rosen. '86.

Soderbergh, Peter A. Women marines. Praeger. '92.

Stiehm, Judith. Arms and the enlisted woman. Temple Univ. Press. '89.

Stremlow, Mary V. Coping with sexism in the military. Rosen. '90.

United States/Congress/House/Committee on Armed Services/ Military Personnel and Compensation Subcommittee. Women in the military. U.S. G.P.O. '90.

United States/Congress/House/Committee on Armed Services/ AFMPZ Special Study Team. An analysis of the effects of varying male and female force levels. Dept. of the Air Force. '85.

United States/Congress/House/Committee on Armed Services/ Military Personnel and Compensation Subcommittee. Parenting issues of Operation Desert Storm. U.S. G.P.O. '91.

Van Devanter, Lynda, with Christopher Morgan. Home before morning; the story of an army nurse in Vietnam. Beaufort. '83.

USA Today. Desert Warriors. Pocket Books. '91.

Walker, Keith. A piece of my heart; the story of 26 American women who served in Vietnam. Presidio Press. '86.

Wekesser, Carol and Polesetsky, Matthew. Women in the military. Greenhaven Press, '91.

White, Anthony G. U.S. servicewomen—academy cadets. Vance Bibliographies. '86.

Whitman, Sylvia. Uncle Sam wants you. Lerner. '93.

Wilden, Anthony. Man and woman, war and peace; the strategist's companion. Routledge and Kegan Paul. '87.

Willenz, June A. Women veterans; America's forgotten heroines. Continuum. '83.

Additional Periodical Articles with Abstracts

For those who wish to read more widely on the subject of women in the military, this section contains abstracts of additonal articles that bear on the topic. Readers who require a comprehensive list of materials are advised to consult the *Reader's Guide to Periodical Literature* and other Wilson indexes.

Combat ban stops women's progress, not bullets. Dusky, Lorraine. *McCalls* 117:26+ My '90

Although women in the U.S. armed forces fill a variety of dangerous roles, they are not allowed to engage in combat. Because promotion is often contingent upon command experience in aircraft, fighting ships, or tanks, servicewomen are denied equal opportunity in the military. A change in this policy can only come from Congress. The results of a national poll on women in combat conducted by McCall's and Democratic representative Patricia Schroeder of Colorado are provided.

Should women have the right to fight?. Barbara Grizzuti Harrison. *Mademoiselle* 96:114 Je '90

Women who wish to participate in combat should be allowed to do so, provided they are aggressive and physically capable. Women may have a positive influence on platoon group dynamics, and the potential romances between platoon mates are no more of a threat than the romances that servicemen have traditionally had with local women. The best scenario of all would be the refusal of both men and women to fight and the end of war in general.

Women in combat. Leslie Morgan. *Seventeen* 49:42 Je '90

Women are still barred from direct combat jobs in the U.S. Army, although during the U.S. invasion of Panama in December they fought and even led men. Women have served in the armed forces since the Revolutionary War, but always in support capacities.

A Mother's duty (servicewomen headed for the Middle East; cover story). *People Weekly* 34:42-9 S 10 '90

The Persian Gulf crisis represents a turning point for the U.S. military, with many mothers and wives being sent overseas. Today, women constitute 11 percent of the nation's 2.1 million active-duty personnel and account for an estimated 11,000 of the 100,000 U.S. troops to be deployed in the Gulf. Virtually no exception is made for women who have children. Several military women's stories are presented.

Black female commander in Saudi Arabia tells how U.S. soldiers adjust to her role. Cynthia Mosely. *Jet* 79:34-5 D 10 '90.

The Army is still adjusting to the presence of women, according to Capt. Cynthia Mosley. Mosley is a black female commander in the U.S. Army in charge of the Alpha Company, the 24th support battalion of the First Army Brigade. The brigade provides supplies to troops in Saudi Arabia. During a recent interview on the MacNeil/Lehrer Newshour, Mosely asserted that women can function well in the Army and are capable of fighting.

Should women fight? Michael Carver Carver. *World Press Review* 37:72 D '90.

An article excerpted from the Independent of London. The view of women's role in the military is undergoing a radical change. Objections to women's place alongside men in combat come from two different camps. The first takes a Victorian view of women as creatures who should be protected; the second shares the age-old prejudice that women are a threat to the inherent purity and intergrity of men. Both of these views patronize women. In fact, women should be treated as the equals of men in the military. Most military combat today does not rely on sheer muscle power and brawn alone. Moreover, if a woman is willing to join the military, she must surely understand that she will face the same risks as her male counterparts do. For the time being, however, because public opinion in Britain opposes women in combat, women should be excluded from posts in which they would be expected to kill, except in self defense. A sidebar offers an opposing viewpoint.

As the war claims its first female M.I.A., Melissa Rathbun-Nealy's pals recall one tough, spirited kid. Ron Arias. *People Weekly* 35:42-3 F 18 '91

Residents of Grand Rapids and Newaygo, Michigan, agree that Army Sp. Melissa Rathbun-Nealy, the first female declared missing in action in the Persian Gulf War, is strong and resourceful, traits they believe will help her survive any ordeal. Rathbun-Nealy, a driver with the 233rd Transportation Company, disappeared after she and Sp. David Lockett became stuck in the sand while driving a flatbed truck near the Kuwaiti border. At the time of their disappearance, Baghdad began to claim that it had captured female prisoners of war, raising the possibility that she had become the first female soldier to fall into Iraqi hands. Rathbun-Nealy is the only daughter of school teachers Joan and Leo Ratbun of Newaygo, a resort town to which they moved from Grand Rapids after they retired. The Rathbuns appreciate the flags and yellow ribbons displayed by friends and current and former neighbors in support of their daughter and all U.S. troops in the war zone.

Survivor of 32 too many Arabian nights, Melissa Rathbun-Nealy heads home from Baghdad. Patricia Freeman. *People Weekly* 35:44-6 Mr 18 '91

Melissa Rathbun-Nealy, the first U.S. servicewoman to be declared missing in action since World War II, is on her way home from Baghdad, thanks to the cease-fire in the Persian Gulf War. Rathbun-Nealy disappeared after her truck got caught in the sand at the Saudi Arabian-Kuwaiti border. She claims that she was treated well by her Iraqi captors and that she spent most of her time during the captivity in isolation.

Inside Iraq, G.I.s bring life where they once dealt death. Bill Hewitt. *People Weekly* 35:88-90 Ap 15 '91

Since the U.S. victory over Iraqi leader Saddam Hussein, U.S. medical units have been working full time to administer care to the war-ravaged residents of southern Iraq. This burden has increased as escalating numbers of Iraqi refugees have fled south to American positions to escape civil war raging elsewhere in Iraq. Compassionate people, such as Sfc. Sylvia Jo Knisley, who commands a 22-member medical platoon, have helped gain the trust of local inhabitants, who were initially wary of the GIs.

Our women at war. Andrea Gross. *Ladies' Home Journal* 108:51-2 Ap '91

Thirty thousand American women are now on duty in the Persian Gulf and are essential to the mission's success. These women fly transport and refueling planes, drive trucks that are full of weapons, pilot transport helicopters, work as mechanics, and stand guard as military police. Several military women in the Gulf are briefly profiled.

War and remembrance. *Ladies' Home Journal* 108:94+ My '91

More than any conflict in decades, the Persian Gulf War affected U.S. women. Women served in the armed forces, waited for loved ones, marched against the war, and died for their country. Six women affected by the war are profiled: Rose Lee Washington, who cared for her grandson while her daughter was in the Gulf; Army Reservists Christine Mayes and Beverly Clark, who were killed by an Iraqi Scud missile; Jody Dumont, who helped design the Patriot missile; Cathy Towsend, the wife of an Air Force pilot; and Diane Mills, who marched against the war while her son, an Air Force Reserve pilot, was in the Gulf.

Should women fight? Even as the Gulf War raged, you said yes. Roxane Farmanfarmaian. *McCall's* 118:50 My '91

In response to a poll conducted by McCall's during the Persian Gulf War, 84 percent of the people questioned said they believed that women should serve in combat positions. The war seemed to strengthen the opinion that women should fight; in a similar poll conducted last year, 79 percent of those questioned gave their approval to the idea of women in combat. Of those questioned who had a daughter, 66 percent said that they would not oppose her going into combat, a 6 percent increase over last year's figure. Other survey results are provided.

Women in the war zone: a look back. *Glamour* 89:105–106+ My '91

The Persian Gulf War was a watershed for women in the military. Composing 6 percent of the U.S. forces in the Gulf, women soldiers resupplied the front lines and flew helicopters on air assaults into enemy territory for the first time. Photographs of women who served in Operation Desert Storm are reproduced.

We are all woman warriors. *Glamour* 89:66 Je '91

The combat exclusion statutes that bar women from frontline military duty restrict female soldiers' opportunities without protecting them from danger. It takes more skill than strength to operate computerized weapons, and trained soldiers have the discipline to keep sexual feelings from getting in the way of duty. In the Persian Gulf War, servicewomen repaired tanks, piloted supplies, trucked ammunition, performed guard duty, and flew helicopters, and a few lost their lives in the line of duty. Nevertheless, even the most skilled female soldiers cannot volunteer for combat duty, and as a result they are unlikely to advance as far as their male counterparts. Ironically, many servicewomen still see their career prospects as superior to those of civilian women, who must contend with a wage gap and daily work-family conflicts.

Senate endorses new SDI plan, wider role for women in combat. Patricia A. Gilmartin. *Aviation Week & Space Technology* 135:7, 24 Ag 5 '91

In debating a $291 billion defense authorization bill for fiscal 1992, the senate has approved provisions that pave the way for vast changes in U.S. anti-military missile research strategy and in the future role of women in the military. The Senate overwhelmingly passed an amendment that would repeal a 1948 law preventing women from flying in combat missions and approved an amendment that calls for the creation of a presidential commission to study the issue of women in combat roles. It also approved a new Strategic Defense Initiative (SDI) architecture that seeks deployment of an anti-ballistic missile system with one or more sites and improved space-based defenses.

Gen. Adams-Ender now top woman in Army as head of Ft. Belvoir in Va. *Jet* 81:8 0 21 91

Brig. Gen. Clara Leach Adams-Ender has been named the new commanding general of Fort Belvoir, a large Army base in Fairfax County, Virginia. A black Army nursing officer with more than 30 years of service, Adams-Ender was formerly the chief of the U.S. Army Nurse Corps. In that job, she directed the efforts of more than 20,000 Army nurses in the Persian Gulf and helped coordinate the operations of more than 25,000 Army medical personnel. According to Democratic representative James P. Moran of Virginia Adams-Ender is now the highest ranking woman in the U.S. Army.

Women in armed forces face frequent sexual harassment *Personnel* 68:16 Mr '91

Reprinted from the Webb Report by Pacific Resource Development Group. A Pentagon study of sexual harassment in the military, which considered responses from over 20,000 men and women, showed that over one-third of the women surveyed experienced some form of direct harassment, including touching, pressure for sexual favors, and rape. In total, about 64 percent said that they had been sexually harassed, either directly or in more subtle ways, such as catcalling, leering, and teasing. Of the males surveyed, 17 percent reported that they had been harassed by male or female personnel.

Night witches, snipers and laundresses. John Erickson. *History Today* 40:29–35 Jl '90

In its desperate fight against the Germans in World War II, the Soviet Union enlisted hundreds of thousands of women in dangerous combat roles. At least 800,000 women served as frontline pilots, navigators, snipers, gunners, paratroopers, tank operators, mine clearers, doctors, nurses, cooks, and laundresses. Thousands more fought with the partisan movement or worked for the underground resistance, while others toiled on the home front as air raid wardens, munitions factory workers, anti-tank ditch diggers, and agricultural workers. Many were honored for their war efforts, and some 88 were awarded the highest Soviet decoration, Hero of the Soviet Union.

Soldier boys, soldier girls. *The New Republic* 202:7–9 F 19 '90

The current debate over opening combat positions to women is shallow and skewed. There is deep oppositon within the Pentagon to women in combat, but it is almost never honestly expressed. Proponents of a fully intergrated military are similarly reluctant to discuss potential pitfalls. The superficiality of the debate is a good argument for going ahead with Rep. Pat Schroeder's plan to allow women to join some Army units in every type of combat specialty on a four-year test basis. It is possible that the presence of women would be debilitating to what military types call the mission, which would be a valid reason for retaining the combat exclusion rule. The only way to really investigate the effects of women in combat, however, is to enter true combat with women in the ranks.

Women in battle. *National Review* 42:18–19 F 5 '90

Despite arguments to the contrary, female soldiers do no belong in combat. Rep. Particia Schroeder and *The New York Times* claim that technological change and social evolution make restrictions on the military use of women unjust and outdated, but their arguments do not stand up to close scrutiny. Few serious armies use women in combat roles. Israel, which drafts most of its young women and uses them in all kinds of military work, has learned from experience to take them out of combat zones. Tests show that few have the upper-body strength required for combat tasks. Keeping combat forces all male would not be discriminatory, as were earlier racial segregation schemes in the military, because men and women are different both physically and psychologically.

A woman's place is at the front. Michael Ryan. *People Weekly* 33:36–41 Ja 22 '90

During the U.S. invasion of Panama, hundreds of female U.S. soldiers received their first taste of combat. Women are still barred from serving in military units designated for combat, but they can serve in support units, such as the Military Police and the Signal Corps, that tend to be drawn quickly into fighting during modern urban warfare. After initially seeming pleased by the attention given to females' accomplishments in the Panamanian conflict, the Army has sought to downplay the issue. Most women who participated in the invasion believe that they made a lasting mark, however. The experiences of several women of the 503rd Military Police Battalion are recounted.

Fire when ready, Ma'am. *Time* 135:29 Ja 15 '90

The exploits of Capt. Linda Bray's Platoon during the U.S. invasion of Panama rekindled a debate over the subject of women and combat. The platoon engaged Panamanian soldiers in a firefight at an attack dog compound near Panama City. U.S. law prohibits women from being assigned to units that are likely to be involved in combat, but activities in Panama proved that the distinction between combat and noncombat situations can easily be blurred. Women like Bray, who is in the military police, are allowed to perform sometimes hazardous support roles.

A fresh shot at full equality. *U.S. News & World Report* 108:12 Ja 15 '90

After seven American women participated in combat during the U.S. invasion of Panama, there was talk in Washington of changing military regulations to allow women a more general combat role. The United States has already revised military rules to open flight training, service academies, and 90 percent of military jobs to women. Democratic representative Patricia Schroeder of Colorado would like the reform to go further. Schroeder has begun to draft legislation that would enable women to serve on a four-year trial basis in Army units that are currently closed to them. Her bill is sure to meet with opposition in the male-dominated Congress and from the military. *Navy Times* reporter Brian Mitchell argues in his new book, *Weak Link*, that women in combat would seriously compromise combat readiness.